# The
# Archaeology
# Workbook

# The Archaeology Workbook

Steve Daniels
&
Nicholas David

EDINBURGH UNIVERSITY PRESS

Edinburgh University Press
22 George Square
Edinburgh

ISBN 0 85224 440 1

Printed in the United States of America

*To Thurstan Shaw*
*Dean of West Africanist archaeologists*
*and to our students*
*at Ibadan, London, and Calgary*

# Contents

# Acknowledgments

The University of Ibadan generously gave us permission to use modified versions of five problems originally set as examinations. We thank our friends and colleagues for ideas and advice given, both in print and in conversation. Louise Baker, Jacquie Hoffman, Kathy Ringer, Persis Clarkson, and Barry MacDonnell all contributed both imagination and skill to their renderings of the figures. Thanks also to Bacon's of Cambridge for a guided tour of their cigar counter.

# Foreword

by
Kent V. Flannery

Each year, several thousand undergraduates in the English-speaking world are exposed to their first courses in archaeology. A handful of these undergraduates go on to pursue an archaeological career. The vast majority, turned off by a lifeless instructor or by endless slides of lifeless potsherds, pursue something else.

Now here is a workbook designed to turn on a few more of those undergraduates and perhaps—just perhaps—seduce a few more of them into archaeology. It is designed to teach them that archaeology is not a subject to be learned by memorization of facts but by solving problems, problems for which there may be no right answer, or for which the right answer might take a whole career to find. In other words, the best kind of problem.

Daniels and David have made this point with humor, which is the most nearly painless way to make it. I give them a high probability of success, because a similar approach was once used by my colleague Henry T. Wright with gratifying results. The problems designed by Wright for Anthropology 221, the University of Michigan's undergraduate Archaeology I course, proved far more popular than any textbook. Like the problems presented by Daniels and David, they gave the undergraduate a sense of participation in the ongoing process of archaeological research.

While the undergraduates may find humor in these workbook exercises, it is satire that will strike the professional archaeologist. I can testify that the background material provided on the archaeology of each area (especially Falasia, Adrar Abu, and Uhuru) sounds very much like actual archaeological site reports I have read—so much so that I may have a hard time keeping a straight face the next time I reread some of the archaeological classics. In particular, the disagreement between Sir Cedric Gardewycket and Dr. Clint P. Trailblazer on the importance of Kwangchung could have come right from the pages of *Antiquity* or *Proceedings of the Prehistoric Society*.

Thus Daniels and David have captured much of the atmosphere of actual archaeology in the manner of ethnologists picking up the mystique of a subculture. They note, among other things, many of the characteristic differences between the way archaeology is taught in Great Britain and in the United States—differences that may be in the process of diminishing due to increased contact and sharing of ideas. The worldwide scope of the problems is a further strength of the book. The ideal should be a problem-solving perspective so fundamentally sound that a student could be parachuted into any archaeological area of the world with trowel and Brunton compass and have some hope of success, regardless of the regional differences.

Realistically, this workbook by itself is not adequate preparation for an actual excavation. On the other hand, it is excellent preparation for a reanalysis of the literature. For example, there are many classic monographs and articles already in print with abundant raw data but little analysis. These data might be profitably reanalyzed by a veteran of these workbook problems. To cite only one example, "The Cemetery of Bilj" made me think of countless mortuary reports still waiting to be studied.

I have only one suggestion for the second edition of *The Archaeology Workbook*. Why not one final problem in which the assignment is not to analyze the archaeological region for which background data is provided but to write a grant proposal to investigate it? Every professional archaeologist invests a great deal of time and energy designing research and trying to convince granting agencies that his proposal will solve problems of significance. Similarly, there is no undergraduate who would not profit from having an instructor critique his first efforts at writing an archaeological research proposal. One could even provide a measure of realism to the exercise by actually "funding" the best proposal to come out of the class. Say, with $35,000 in Monopoly money?

Kent V. Flannery
University of Michigan

# A Preface
# for Instructors

This book began as an experiment devised by Steve Daniels as part of a course entitled "The historical interpretation of archaeological data," intended for second-year undergraduates in the newly founded Department of Archaeology at the University of Ibadan, Nigeria. The course at first followed the traditional lecture and tutorial format, the only innovation being that the final exam was a problem, made up for the occasion, that required the students to *apply* their knowledge. The students' performances turned out to be well below their potential, and this led to the confection of further problems given as assignments and discussed in class. Instead of being brought down from on high, method and theory began to be generated in the heat of argument, guided and controlled by the instructor. The students not only enjoyed the course more but markedly improved their grasp of archaeological reasoning. They learned to consult the authorities on methodological questions with a specific application in mind, rather than in order to memorize generalizing dogma, and they proved more enthusiastic and critical in their other courses. The success of this approach led to the development of the present workbook.

Whatever their familiarity with secondary sources and theoretical issues, most archaeology students gain little experience analyzing and integrating real data during their undergraduate years, or at best their experience is limited to materials from a particular area or period. This common defect in the design of degree courses is predetermined by the archaeological literature and the nature of archaeology itself. Problems on which data are easily available tend to be either too complex or too trivial for pedagogical purposes. Original materials are scattered in a variety of monographs and specialist journals, often in more than one language. It becomes difficult in practice and prohibitively expensive to provide students with real data on which to cut their teeth.

*The Archaeology Workbook* is designed for students with a basic grounding in archaeological theory and method. That is to say, they have worked their way through a good introductory text and have been exposed to basic concepts, discussion of the nature of the archaeological record, and the most commonly used methods and techniques for the collection and analysis of data. They are aware of the importance of context, and even if they could not get an A for an essay on "The Concept of Type," they do know that classification makes comparison possible and that the particular approach employed should be attuned to the problem under study. They can also read a section or a distribution map and understand the principles of relative dating. We also expect a critical understanding of radiocarbon dates, their probabilistic nature, and the factors affecting their validity. Calibration can, however, safely be ignored. Students should also be familiar with simple ecological, economic, and chronological reasoning based on evidence from geology, botany, and zoology. Where knowledge of, for example, the nature and habits of a particular species is assumed by us but unknown to the student, a little library research is all that is needed —and will do no harm. No statistical skills are necessary beyond an ability to handle percentages and construct simple contingency tables.

Although the problems are set in various parts of the world and in different periods, students need not know the details of regional prehistory. We have avoided local technicalities and jargon. A previous acquaintance with the outlines of world prehistory or those of a major culture area will, on the other hand, help to provide an understanding of the kinds of explanation and reconstruction most commonly offered. We have attempted to order the problems so that they become progressively more difficult through the book, but it should be realized that the degree of difficulty depends in part upon the students' previous training. Composition of answers to the first nine problems should not require more than two to four hours of a student's time, but the last four (10–13) are quite a bit harder.

The problems are designed to familiarize the students with a wide but still limited range of issues. Numbers 1, 2, 4, 7, 9, and 11 are exercises in the use of varying combinations of stratigraphic, typological, locational, chronometric, biological, linguistic, and historical evidence. In each the student is asked to construct or modify on the basis of new data an outline culture history of a little-known region and to identify the culture processes involved. These vary from problem to problem. Thus in *Falasia* the student will, among other things, be concerned with the respective roles of migration and indigenous development, while the *Adrar Abu* calls for interpretation of faunal assemblages and of rock art. Problem 3, *The Island of Coolay*, is one of research design in a context of "cultural resource management." It is thus in a sense the obverse of Problems 1, 2, and 4 and has been placed early in the book to emphasize the critical importance of this aspect of archaeological inquiry and to assist the student in evaluating the potential and limitations of other data sets. Problems 5, 6, 8, 10, 12, and 13 are more precisely oriented to a variety of data sets and approaches. The seriation of pottery from *Petristan* reveals structuring by time, space, and other variables. In the *Sierra de la Serenidad*, different modes of production help to account for the observed distribution of artifacts, while activities and cultural style both influence the prehistoric record of the *Pitts River Basin. The Lon Gon Bronzes* are a source of controversy in the world of art history; can archaeology solve the problem? Ethnicity, age, sex, craft, and social status are all expressed, albeit imperfectly, in a sample of twenty burials from the *Cemetery of Bilj*. And in *New Frisia* archaeology is able to complement the Europocentric historical record by documenting the contrasting impacts of Spanish and Dutch colonists on the indigenous Amerindian population.

Before they start, students should read the Introduction, as this describes the conventions adopted by the authors and gives advice on approaches to problem solving. We give a sample student's answer to *Falasia* and append comments that point out many of the more common errors and ways to avoid them. A sample instructor's answer is also given that will perhaps prove useful as a model; we have again commented on unstated assumptions, points missed, and alternative interpretations.

However ingenious, problems of this kind have obvious limitations as teaching devices, and the authors are themselves constrained by the genre. The constraints arise largely from our attempt to make the problems general and accessible to a wide range of students, who may or may not be enrolled in formal courses of instruction. They are intended to be useful not only to budding archaeologists but also to others such as historians who may find themselves using archaeological interpretations while having little or no experience of the way such conclusions are derived from the data. We have therefore omitted many lines of evidence that seem to us to require more specialized knowledge. Others, such as historical linguistics, oral traditions, textual evidence, and faunal and floral data, are presented in a predigested or uncritically accepting form. Also predigested, in nearly every case, is the typological evidence, partly because the addition of typological ambiguities would have made our problems too long and complex, but even more because we feel that typological skills and sophistication can best be acquired by handling real objects in the laboratory in the context of real problems, not from looking at pictures on a page.

The emphasis on generality has also led us to omit various specialized fields within archaeology. Industrial and underwater investigations, ethnoarchaeology, taphonomy, and astro-archaeology have their own interpretative and procedural problems with which we do not expect the average student to be familiar. For similar reasons none of the problems is concerned uniquely with the Stone Age, nor does our framework allow space to deal with more than single aspects of complex societies. We have, on the other hand, included a problem in historical archaeology, because we feel that this field belongs properly to the mainstream of archaeology to which it is at last showing signs of making unique contributions.

The problems are designed to simulate real-life situations. The evidence presented is incomplete, of varying and often doubtful validity, and may or may not be strictly relevant. The questions are open ended; there are no right answers, only constructions of varying levels of plausibility. Although we had particular historical scenarios in mind when we wrote them, we have found in practice that students and colleagues will vigorously propose and successfully defend quite different reconstructions. Indeed it is our experience that much of the value of the problems lies not merely in the formulation of an explanation, but in criticism and defense during group discussion of various different interpretations of the same data. One advantage of fictitious data emerges here; nobody can be an expert able to draw on more information, and this promotes much freer and less self-conscious interaction. The instructor can, of course, raise the level of argument by introducing relevant theory and comparative material.

The levels at which the problems may prove useful vary widely. Although, as we have said, the average student will probably not have the background to benefit much before the second year of a university degree program that starts from scratch, there is nothing that makes them inherently unsuitable for secondary or high school students participating in a general archaeology course. An instructor can, of course, adjust the level of difficulty to his students' abilities and experience by briefing them on aspects of the problems before they are attempted. At the other end of the scale, we have found that the harder problems make instructive and stimulating assignments for postgraduate seminars and have ourselves learned from them about our own theoretical and political attitudes and preconceptions.

Finally, and in self defense, we give notice that we will not enter into correspondence about *answers,* but would, on the other hand, be glad to entertain problems for possible inclusion in future editions of *The Archaeology Workbook.*

# An Introduction
# for Students

In setting these problems, we first thought of issues or topics in which students require practical training, the integration of archaeological and other data, for example, or modes of production and distribution, or "horizontal stratigraphy." Then we decided on a particular plot or structure of events and the factors that brought them about, then on an area in which they might have taken place. Finally, after consulting the literature for "local color," we fleshed out the plot and transformed it into data such as might have been recovered by archaeologists and specialists in related fields. But this does *not* mean that you can reverse the process, work backwards and arrive at a solution identical to our original scenario in which groups of people, variously motivated, do different things at different times and places. There are several reasons for this, and they are worth understanding because they apply in real archaeological situations where the plot is provided not by Daniels and David but by God, the force of history, Great Men, or the unfolding logic of systemic evolution.

First, and very practically, there is the matter of data recovery. The material manifestations of cultural systems do not simply subside into the ground when their useful life is over; they are *transformed* into potential archaeological data by both natural and cultural formation processes and may then be *sampled* by an archaeologist, or indeed by a grave robber. Preservation varies from layer to layer, site to site, and region to region. Techniques of recovery are constantly improving; excavators also vary enormously in their expertise. Thus in any one area, besides the latest high-powered but still imperfect monograph, you will find scrappy but vital reports of digs carried out in ways that we would now characterize as criminal. The analyst is constantly having to make use of information of uneven quality, even if all the data are drawn from the same "homogeneous" culture.

Second, even in the best studied areas, the data represent only a tiny fraction of its past peoples' activities. Many recent developments in archaeological method are aimed at ensuring that this fraction is as representative as possible of the range of past behaviors originally present. Research design is or should be directed towards ensuring that the analyses carried out are efficient, in that they are adequate to solve the immediate problems, while not being unnecessarily time consuming or expensive. Neither should they prejudice any further analyses that may foreseeably be required at a later stage in research. The typological and other "predigested" data, on physical anthropology for example, that you will meet with in the problems are for the most

5

part of the simplest kind, as is appropriate in little-known areas where the prehistorian is concerned with blocking out a picture of the past, rather than in refining the details of a particular segment. In any one problem we can only provide you with a few sites and limited range of fossilized activities. Although we have constructed the data so that there are linkages suggesting certain interpretations (as may well not be the case in real life), you should never forget that you are dealing with a small sample subject to unknown biases. As you will later find when faced with real data, inferences must be made on the basis of inadequate evidence, including others' work that you may consider invalid in whole or in part but which for practical reasons cannot be checked. A good archaeologist learns to accept this and defines areas of ignorance and uncertainty, specifying how these might be reduced by further work.

Third, there are the limitations of archaeological theory. Lewis Binford once wrote that "The practical limitations of our knowledge of the past are not inherent in the nature of the archaeological record; the limitations lie in our methodological naiveté, in our lack of development for principles determining the relevance of archaeological remains to propositions regarding processes and events of the past."* This is an inspiring if extreme view. Neither in archaeology nor in the many other disciplines on which it depends has either theory or practice reached the required degree of perfection. We are still remarkably naive, perhaps not surprisingly, since most archaeologists are working with the material remains of cultures they have not and cannot experience directly even if, as anthropologists, they do attempt to immerse themselves in relevant comparative materials. But much uncontrolled archaeological inference is still founded upon "common sense," often merely another way of describing ethnocentric preconceptions.

In a moment we will tell you about the conventions we have followed in formulating the problems and offer advice as to how to approach them. Before doing so, we should, if not agree on, at least bring to your attention the different vocabularies or sets of concepts used to describe archaeological entities. The British write, for example, of "assemblages," "industries," and "cultures"; French authors of "outillages" or "séries," "industries," and "civilisations," "industries" having a different range of meanings in the two languages. The worst definition of an industry was, as one might expect, dreamed up by a committee that defined it as "represented by all the known objects that a group of prehistoric people manufactured in one area over some span of time." This begs so many questions as to be completely useless, although it is still applied by some Africanist archaeologists to entities as different as the Acheulian and the Nigerian Nok "culture" (itself an inappropriate term in this instance!). Just as there is no *one* right typology but a variety of approaches that can profitably be employed at different stages of research, so it is unreasonable to expect that the same analytical concepts will fit both the Mousterian of the Mediterranean basin and the Classic of Oaxaca. In preparing your answers, you will have to choose a set that suits the problem. Although you probably already have been exposed to this aspect of archaeo-

---

*L. R. Binford, Archaeological perspectives. In *New perspectives in archaeology.* ed. S. R. Binford and L. R. Binford (Chicago/New York: Aldine, 1968), p. 23.

logical theory, you may find the two sets of concepts given below to be of some use, especially if you are not receiving formal instruction. They should at least discourage you from thinking and writing about undefined entities such as "the people" or even "they." Variants of the first set, extracted with modifications from D. L. Clarke's *Analytical Archaeology* (London: Methuen, 1968) are used by many British writers:

Attribute: a logically irreducible character such as length

Artifact: any object modified by a set of humanly imposed attributes

Artifact type: a population of artifacts that shares a recurring range and combination of attributes

Assemblage: an associated set of "contemporary" artifacts

Culture: a polythetic* set of artifact types that consistently recurs together in assemblages

Culture group: a family of related cultures, characterized by assemblages sharing a polythetic range of different varieties of the same artifact types

Technocomplex: a group of much more distantly or unrelated cultures sharing the same general families of artifact types as a widely diffused and interlinked response to common factors in environment, economy, and technology

There are obviously several questions raised by these definitions, for example, the meanings of "contemporary" or "family." The second set, adapted from G. R. Willey's and P. Phillips's *Method and Theory in American Archaeology* (Chicago: University of Chicago Press, 1958), has the advantage that the archaeological entities are defined with reference to a previously given spatial framework. The time frame may be either relative or absolute, but the duration of specific units or series will depend upon rates of culture change.

Spatial divisions

Site: a variable area (camp to city) more or less continuously covered with archaeological remains that pertain to a single unit of settlement. . . . the basic unit for stratigraphic studies. Cultural changes result from the passage of time.

Locality: a variable area not larger than the space that might be occupied by a single community or local group and small enough to permit the *working assumption* of complete cultural homogeneity at any given time

Region: likely to coincide with a major physiographic subdivision in which at a given time a high degree of cultural homogeneity may be expected but not counted on. . . . the space that might be occupied by a social unit larger than the community, possibly the "tribe" or society

---

*A group is polythetic if each of its members possesses many but not all group characteristics, each characteristic is possessed by many members, and no single characteristic is diagnostic of group membership.

Area: corresponds roughly to the "culture area" of the ethnographer and tends to coincide with major physiographic regions

Basic Archaeological units

Component: the archaeological materials found in a single level of a single site, the manifestation of a given phase at a single site

Phase: a unit possessing traits sufficiently characteristic to distinguish it from all other units similarly conceived, whether of the same or other cultures or civilizations, spatially limited to a locality or region and chronologically limited to a relatively brief interval of time

Culture and Civilization: reflect the major segments of culture history. . . . groups of phases

Temporal series

Local sequence: a chronological series of components or phases within the geographical limits of a locality

Regional sequence: a chronological series of phases within the limits of a region, arrived at by correlating (and not by combining or conflating) local sequences

Integrative units

Horizon: a primarily spatial continuity represented by one or more cultural traits whose nature and mode of occurrence permit the assumption of a broad and rapid spread

Tradition: a primarily temporal continuity represented by persistent configurations in single technologies or other systems of related forms

This abbreviated listing cannot fairly represent Willey's and Phillips's thought; for example, they insist that "the concept of phase has no appropriate scale independent of the cultural situation in which it is applied." This may be taken as generally true of the other entities; the Acheulian cleaver may have taken tens, even hundreds, of thousands of years to spread over large areas of the Old World, tobacco pipes only a hundred years or so, but both are used as horizon styles. You may find it useful to make a diagram showing the relationships of the different concepts and to consider whether others might not sometimes be needed. A level may contain materials of varying ages; should these be described as a component? If a community regularly moves between winter and summer camps, fishing in one and hunting in the other, might it not be appropriate to distinguish the resulting components (or assemblages) as "facies" of the same phase? And so on.

But let us now get down to cases. You will note that the problems are set in different parts of the world, some of which may be unfamiliar to you. Don't lose heart; only the cultural vocabulary changes, the syntax of archaeology remains the same. You should be able to apply your knowledge of the discipline in any area. We have tried to achieve a degree of verisimilitude in all the problems. Although the settings, events, and materials are fictional, they or others quite like them could have occurred in the region in which they are set. So before starting a problem, feel free but not obliged to consult a secondary source on the area. Although unnecessary, knowledge of the area and period in question will be a help rather than a hindrance, and you will learn a little world prehistory on the side. When, on the other hand, we refer to real peoples, personages, or places—the Chinese, King Philip of Spain, or Carthage—their behavior is true to their historical character even if it never actually happened. (Should you not be able to distinguish between our creations and the historical residue, you have gained the chance to expand your general knowledge!)

You have, of course, read the Instructors' Preface and have learned that several of the early problems involve reconstruction of the culture history of an area. You are being asked to do what was done for you in the first lecture you went to on Mesopotamia or in that chapter on the Andes in the world prehistory text. How do you set about this? First, it is important that you pay attention to *all* the data given even if, upon reflection, you decide to discard some as irrelevant. The text, tables, and figures supply complementary information and are not there merely for decoration. After studying the data carefully, the next step is to establish a geographical and chronological framework. There is no point in talking about how various events and activities are related economically, socially, or otherwise until you have decided that they were near enough in space and time to have been related at all. Consider the geography. Examine the area and if possible subdivide it into regions that are ecologically distinct, within each of which people might at any one time have followed the same way of life. Regions that are ecologically similar but widely separated on the ground are best treated as quite different. Then start to construct the chronology. This is easiest to do one region at a time, and if there are enough sites, one locality at a time, starting with the site that has produced the finest stratigraphy. The suggested procedure for each region is as follows:

Take a sheet of rough paper and draw vertical time columns for each site, "Late" at the top and "Early" at the bottom, and a summary column for the region. Scale the columns to cover the period under study. Enter at the appropriate points any exact dates for historical events. Then enter estimates, such as radiocarbon dates, using some device, perhaps a vertical line representing the standard error, to show the relative uncertainty. Do not forget that, quite apart from any statistical uncertainty, you should determine whether the samples are likely to be genuinely associated with what they purport to date, and that errors can arise from faulty procedures in the field and in the laboratory. Opposite the dates you can place any economic, typological, climatic, or other information to which the dates refer. When all "absolute" dates are in, information for which there are only relative dates can be added. The time columns, prepared locality by locality, and the region column are now a first approximation to a chronology. If your choice of regions has been good, the chronology of any one region is likely to be fairly simple, assuming, of course, that the data are there with which to build it. If you find that closely comparable events occur at very different times in parts of the same region, then your initial choice may have been poor, some dates are perhaps misleading, or you may be dealing with an historical process. Note and mark any discrepancies but leave making final decisions on them until a later stage.

When you have time columns for each region, they can be compared with the aim of building up an overall framework. If there are no clear groupings of components into phases and of phases into cultures that can be correlated from locality to locality and from region to region, you may find it helpful to subdivide the time span into "periods," a general purpose term conveniently employed in early stages of research. Periods are best chosen so that similar conditions of life prevailed throughout any one, though periods defined only by major or easily recognizable events at the start and finish can also be useful. Periodization in part depends upon availability of data; a different selection of sites for excavation might, and probably would, have suggested an alternative scheme.

Major events and periods can be correlated from region to region to produce a connected areal chronology, bearing in mind that the dates of particular events may indeed differ from one region to another, for reasons that you are invited to infer. Throughout the process of establishing a framework, you will find discrepancies and contradictions and will have to decide whether these are real and require historical explanation, or are mere artifacts of research. If they are real, can you account for the discrepancy? Several reconstructions and thorough checks against the details of the evidence may be required before you reach a framework you find convincing. Even then, as with real archaeological problems, loose ends may remain that cannot be explained.

Once you have decided on a framework, it should be much easier to examine each region at a particular period and try to group the phases and to reconstruct the economic, social, and political system or systems within it. If you think a system is sufficiently homogeneous, you may wish to give it a cultural name, usually based upon a "type site" at which it was first recognized or is best expressed. Or again your reconstruction of one aspect may send you back to alter the main time and space framework. You may, for instance, find that some class of artifact is not representative of a separate culture but of a particular economic activity, or that what you had provisionally identified as a political entity makes better sense as a trade route. Understanding patterns and processes in the past depends to a considerable extent upon your knowledge of comparable patterns and processes documented by prehistorians, ethnographers, and others—including those you observe in your daily life. Do not therefore regard any of the problems as capsules set apart from your other courses and experience; bring all your knowledge into play. And finally, however attractive you find your own reconstruction, you should not accept it wholeheartedly (if at all!) until you have examined alternatives and decided that, for specific reasons, they are definitely less satisfactory. Sometimes it is best not to plump for any one solution but to leave the final answer as a probability balanced among several possibilities. In any case, you should indicate how reliable you consider your reconstruction to be and suggest what further work would help to resolve outstanding uncertainties.

The preceding paragraphs should help you come to grips with problems like number 3, in which you are asked to design a plan of research for Coolay in order to generate the structured data that will make possible the drawing of valid inferences about the island's early history. As time and space are the dimensions of the contextual frame within which archaeological data are interpreted, the advice given is relevant in the other problems as well. Some of these are more narrowly focused, but the same principles are involved. Reference to an introductory text on method and theory for help on specific points, combined with some thought on your part, will supply any extra equipment needed to "solve" the problems. We are throwing you into the middle of the pool, not the deep end, and your toes can touch bottom.

Archaeology is a bit like a three-dimensional crossword puzzle with several clues missing, some answers in an unknown language, and a frame that changes as you move from one level to another. We enjoy it and hope that you do, too.

# PROBLEM

# 1

# Falasia

**INSTRUCTIONS:** Study the background information and archaeological data. Then write, as concisely as possible, a reconstruction of the prehistory of Falasia. State clearly the reasoning behind your interpretations and how much confidence you would place in your conclusions. You may also indicate what further research you regard as critical to answer important questions left open by the data to hand.

**BACKGROUND INFORMATION:** Falasia is a country in the southern temperate latitudes of Africa (fig. 1.1). It is divided into two major environmental zones by the Garna Mountains, which run from northwest to southeast. To the east of the mountains, the land falls slowly to the sea, and broad rivers, such as the Anara and the Bunyip, supply water to fertile plains. The annual rainfall is 42 inches and the vegetation chiefly open savanna. To the west of the Garna range, the land falls rapidly to the sea, and rivers are small, fast running, and often seasonal. The soil is reasonably fertile but subject to serious erosion during the short and violent rainy season. The annual rainfall is 16 inches, and the vegetation is mostly thorn-scrub.

Falasia is poor in mineral resources; while low-grade iron ore is plentiful, no sources of copper are known.

To the west of the mountains, the main language spoken today is Sirewa, while the common tongue in eastern Falasia is Chifala. A recent linguistic study has shown that while Sirewa and Chifala are members of the same language family, the differences between them suggest that they separated some 4,000 years ago.

Oral tradition among Sirewa-speaking groups does not go back beyond 200 years, but the Sirewa claim that their ancestors have always lived in their present area. Chifala traditions tell of their arrival from a homeland in the north, in the neighboring Republic of Zaronia, and their settlement south of the river Bunyip about 800 years ago.

The following is a quotation from the journal of Cornelius Brent, a European trader whose visit to Falasia in 1473 provides the first written reference to the country: "Sailing to the north we came to the mouth of a river which the natives call Anara. At first they would not trade with us, but after messengers from the King of that region had visited us and been shown to what uses bronze could be put, they shewed a prodigious interest in the metal and we were able to do good trade in fine ivory."

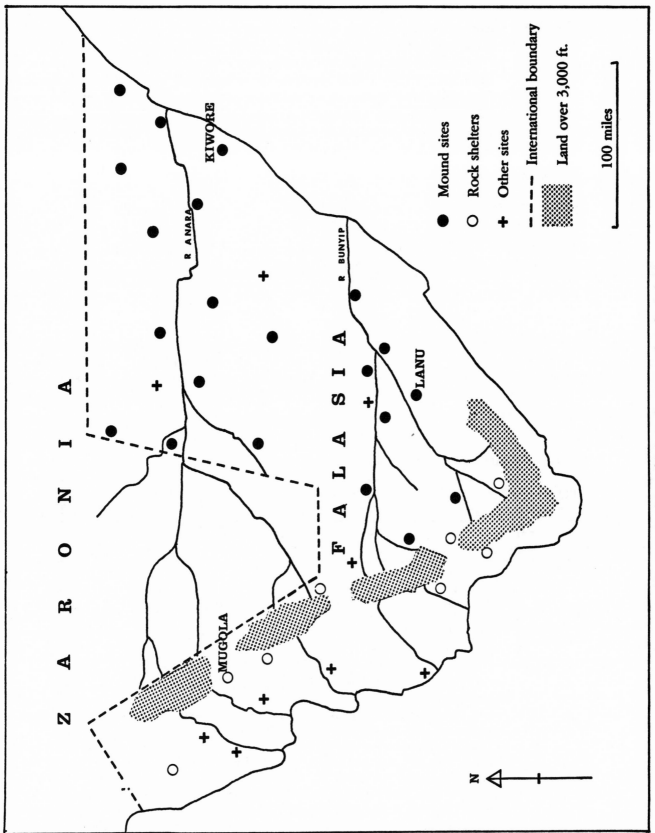

Figure 1.1. Map of Falasia showing archaeological sites

**ARCHAEO-LOGICAL DATA:** Archaeological work in Falasia has only recently begun, but during the last five years two research projects have been carried out. The State Archaeological Survey has worked extensively in eastern Falasia, while a visiting expedition from the Grond Museum has been operating west of the Garna range. Both have involved field reconnaissance and study of aerial photographs. Many sites have been located and three excavations conducted, at Kiwore, Lanu, and Mugola. The following tables (tables 1.1 and 1.2), section (fig. 1.2), distribution maps (figs. 1.3 and 1.4) and accompanying notes give some of the results of this work.

**TABLE 1.1.   Dates and main finds from Trench A at Kiwore**

| | POTTERY WARES (percent.) | | | OTHER FINDS (No. of specimens) | | C¹⁴ DATES | MATERIAL DATED |
|---|---|---|---|---|---|---|---|
| Level | RED WARE | BLACK WARE | OTHER | BRONZE OBJECTS | IMPORTED GLASS | | |
| 1 | 89 | 1 | 10 | 24 | — | | |
| 2 | 94 | — | 6 | 10 | 1 | $1450 \pm 80$ A.D. | Charcoal |
| 3 | 82 | 2 | 16 | 3 | — | $1500 \pm 80$ A.D. | Charcoal |
| 4 | 39 | 47 | 14 | — | — | | |
| 5 | 4 | 89 | 7 | — | — | $980 \pm 110$ A.D. | Charcoal |
| 6 | — | 83 | 17 | — | — | $450 \pm 120$ A.D. | Charcoal |
| 7 | — | 86 | 14 | — | — | $500 \pm 600$ A.D. | Bone collagen |
| 8 | — | — | — | — | — | $100 \pm 150$ B.C. | Charcoal |

**TABLE 1.2.   Dates and main finds from Trench F at Lanu**

| | POTTERY WARES (percent.) | | | OTHER FINDS (No. of specimens) | | C¹⁴ DATES | MATERIAL DATED |
|---|---|---|---|---|---|---|---|
| Level | RED WARE | BLACK WARE | OTHER | BRONZE OBJECTS | IMPORTED GLASS | | |
| 1 | 84 | — | 16 | 7 | 3 | | |
| 2 | 81 | — | 19 | 18 | 1 | | |
| 3 | 89 | 3 | 8 | 20 | — | $1620 \pm 90$ A.D. | Charcoal |
| 4 | 81 | 6 | 13 | 14 | 2 | | |
| 5 | — | 74 | 26 | — | — | $1300 \pm 90$ A.D. | Charcoal |
| 6 | — | 85 | 15 | — | — | | |

**Notes**

In addition to the finds shown in the tables above, a small number of iron implements, including hoes, were found at all levels at Lanu and Levels 1 to 7 at Kiwore. Carbonized traces of millet grains were found in a number of sherds of Black Ware. Red Ware was occasionally decorated with maize cobs in Level 1 at Kiwore and Levels 1 and 2 at Lanu.

No figures are yet available for animal bones at Lanu. At Kiwore bones of wild animals decrease from 100% in Level 8 to about 10% in Levels 5 and above, while bones of domestic animals (chiefly cattle and goat) increase from 25% in Level 7 to 90% in Level 5.

Level 8 at Kiwore contained a number of chipped stone tools, including small arrowheads.

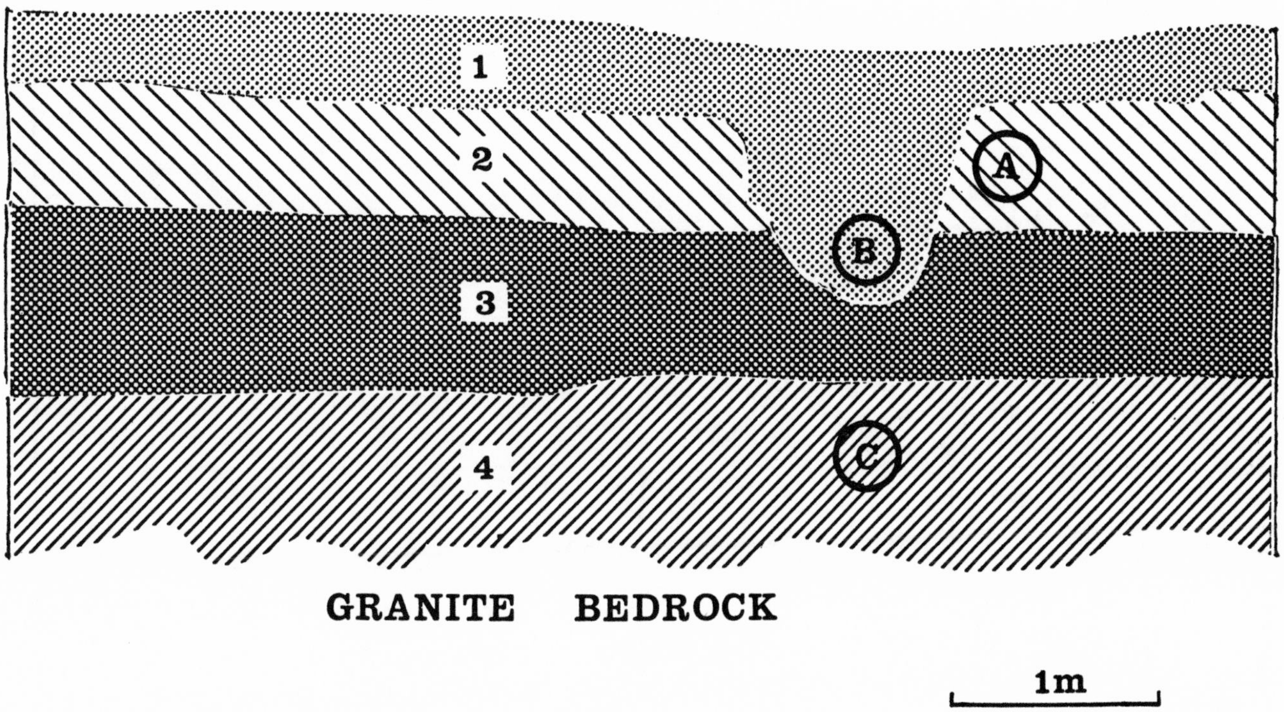

**Figure 1.2.** Section of the north side of the main trench at Mugola rock shelter

## Notes on Figure 1.2.

KEY TO STRATIGRAPHY

Layer 1. Dark ashy deposit containing mostly grey pottery with a little Black Ware similar to that from Kiwore. Bones of domestic goat and occasional cow. An iron axe and an imported glass bead.

Layer 2. Pinkish cave earth with grey pottery and Black Ware. Bones of goat and wild antelope. Two iron arrowheads.

Layer 3. Red cave earth. Chipped stone tools and a few ground stone axes. Two sherds of Black Ware. Bones of wild antelope.

Layer 4. Red claylike deposit with small boulders of decomposing granite. Chipped stone tools including many small arrowheads. Bones of wild antelope.

RADIOCARBON DATES

Three charcoal samples were taken from the points indicated by the appropriate letter on the section drawing. The dates are as follows:

A. 1500 ± 90 A.D.

B. 1700 ± 80 A.D.

C. 500 ± 150 B.C.

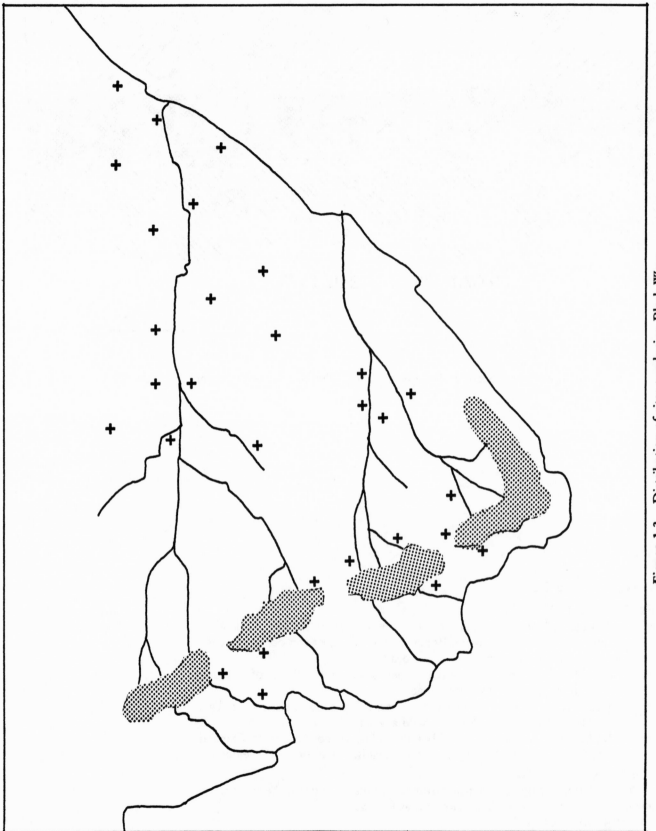

Figure 1.3.    Distribution of sites producing Black Ware

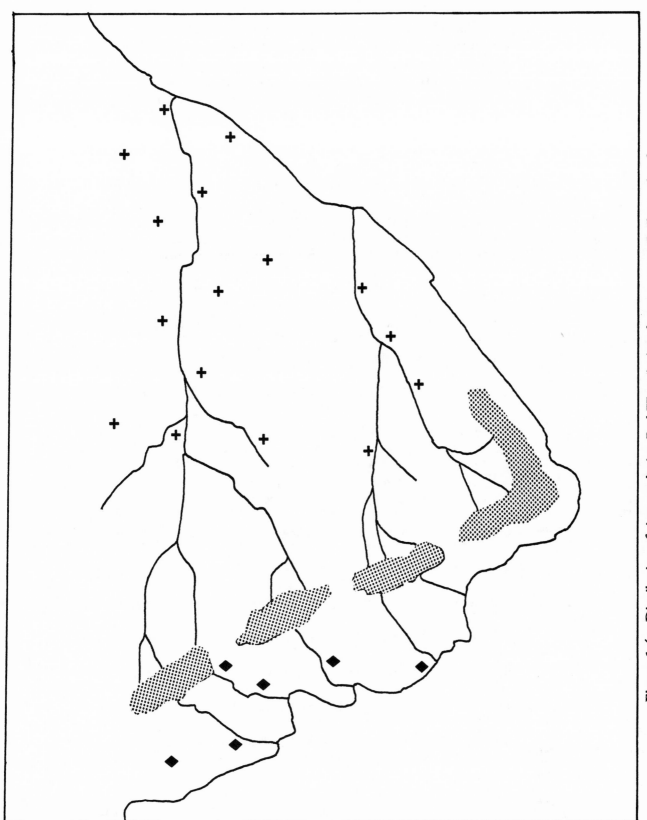

Figure 1.4. Distribution of sites producing Red Ware (+) and grey pottery similar to that from Mugola rock shelter (◆)

## A STUDENT'S ANSWER WITH INSTRUCTOR'S COMMENTS

This "student's answer" is in fact a compilation of several written by students in the penultimate year of an archaeology degree course. It is in no way a caricature but typical of answers received from students who have had courses in theory and method, world prehistory, and at least one area course besides some fieldwork experience, but who have never been faced with the problem of turning raw archaeological data into a coherent picture of the past.

**COMMENTS**

*You mean that no sites of this age have yet been found—they may well be.*

*This "date" is derived from the linguistic evidence (presumably glottochronological); say so, and treat it with the utmost caution.*

*Don't use linguistic labels for arch. entities. Basis for this correlation?*

*You have a sample of 2 dates only for the preceramic Late Stone Age—quite insufficient on which to base such a statement.*

*i.e., nomadic hunter/gatherers who made use of rock shelters and open sites, and who do not on present evidence appear to be regionally differentiated.*

*This date with its huge standard error is virtually useless. Say rather that "Pottery first appears in the arch. record in the 1st half of the 1st millennium A.D."*

*These statements conflict and neither is supported by the data. Since a whole new complex appears and is unlikely to have come by sea, a general N → S movement is likely.*

*Surely the pottery-making, iron-working/using + agricultural complex arrives fully formed?*

*No evidence of this and most Africanists would hotly dispute it.*

*There is no necessary progression from stone to metal (and in fact there is no Bronze Age in sub-Saharan Africa).*

*The immigrants may well have incorporated the previous occupants of E. Falasia. Or could they? Evidence on this point?*

*You mean herding and stock-breeding—the domestication had occurred elsewhere.*

**STUDENT'S ANSWER**    *Regions?*

About 4,000 years ago no human inhabited the lands of Falasia, but after that time a people whom I will call the proto-Sirewa began to enter Falasia from the *Perhaps, but no evidence of this* northwest. Internal conflicts had forced them to migrate southwards. After initial penetration it took the proto-Sirewa about 500 years (dates of 500 ± 150 and 100 ± 150 B.C.) to spread throughout all the country. It would appear that the people were at a preceramic, nondomesticated technological level and hunted and gathered their food from sources nearby.

No pottery existed in the NE before 500 ± 600 A.D., but then as the years *meaning?* passed by the people began to develop a more "sophisticated" culture. At this point in time the Black Ware people began to come down from NE Falasia to *pottery = people? What else characterizes phase?* the area of what is now the Kiwore site. The sites seem to be in an east to west progression. They originally settled along the Anara and Bunyip rivers and only later moved into the remote interior. The people began to domesticate plants and animals, namely millet and goats. This development could only have been the result of influence from the North of Africa. Since no copper is present in the area, it would have been impossible to make bronze, so iron instruments succeeded the stone industry. Due to the more efficient technological level of the Black Ware people, they had little difficulty in pushing out the proto-Sirewans.

With regard to animal domestication at the Kiwore site, when related to pottery, a shift may be detected in the type of animals utilized. A transitional period may be said to exist of about 400 years for levels 5 to 7. This transition

*Better phrased as "increasing reliance being placed on domestic stock at the expense of hunting."*

*Level 6; your "transition" is complete by level 5 times.*

indicates a change from hunting to domestication (level 7: 25% domestic and

75% wild animals as opposed to 90% domestic and 10% wild in level 5). In

other words the domestication of animals by the B. W. people becomes greater

*How?*

and greater. The pottery trends support this, and are part of what may be called

a sedentary stage.

*Which you should define in terms of all its characteristic features.*

Black Ware and its predominance in Level 7 coincides with the beginning

of the sedentary culture at Kiwore. The "development" of Red Ware may be

*Is it a development, the diffusion of a new ware or what?*

said to correspond with the next stage in this sedentary period, and it is logical

to assume that it is a better grade than the black. The new red ware was

*Logical perhaps but by no means necessarily true, e.g., the quality of pottery in sub-Sah. Africa generally deteriorates from "Neolithic" to Iron Age.*

introduced, along with the cultivation of maize by proto-Chifala people (oral

*A New World crop, must be later than A.D. 1500*

tradition) who seem to have driven the Black Ware people west across the

*English!*

*A dramatic interpretation based upon 1) an oral trad. which even if accurate may well only refer to part of the community, and 2) a change in ware but not other aspects of culture. Alternative suggestions?*

mountains where they seem to have cohabited with the Grey Ware people

(another lot of proto-Sirewa who began to develop their own style of pottery)

for a time and then either assimilated or died out. Since pottery is the only

*Now you have me confused— are the Sirewa the product of a fusion of Late Stone Age + Black Ware peoples, or is the contribution of the B. W. people insignificant? What if anything correlates with the appearance of grey ware?*

indicator for this theory, its presence may instead mean only trade. The proto-

*How do you decide between these alternatives? Argue the case for each.*

Chifala Red Ware people remained E of the mountains probably because of the

*A monstrous linguistic-ceramic people—why not simply "Kiwore culture, phase 2?"*

more desirable climate and topography.

*i.e., better suited to their mixed farming adaptation.*

It is at about this time (1473 A.D.) that the first historic contacts take place.

This is nicely shown by the presence of bronze and glass trade goods at Kiwore

*Yes—good*

in levels 1 through 3, although there is something funny about the date for level

*No: no conflict even at 1 standard error.*

2 which should be later. Bronze and glass were traded between Kiwore and

*No: the 2 site sample suggests an exchange network of some kind, but not necessarily direct Kiwore-Lanu connections.*

Lanu.

As to Lanu, this site may be said to be merely an extension of the findings

*You miss the point—comparison of the sequences is required to generate a provisional sequence for E. Falasia.*

at Kiwore. Level 6 roughly corresponds to level 5 at Kiwore. Level 5 at Kiwore

indicates a transitionary period, as has been mentioned, denoting animal domes-

*Good—you are at least trying to correlate part of the sequences. But Lanu level 6 could be as early as Kiwore 7, or correlate with several of the lower Kiwore levels. And why does Red Ware appear later at Lanu than at K.?*

tication and the early stages of agriculture. Black Ware is present (89%) and,

**?**

not surprisingly, it's 85% in level 6 of Lanu. It may also be suggested that some

wild animal bones would be found at Lanu (tho' only a small amount). The Lanu

*meaning ??*

people had prior knowledge of Kiwore pottery, and probably of animal and

plant domestication as well; subsequently, wild animals could have served as a

minor supplement.

Contact may be suggested to have occurred between the Black Ware

people (Kiwore level 5) and Mugola level 3, a site that is proto-Sirewa in nature.

This level contains Black ware, and this is further suggested by the fact that iron

*1–6 only! Careless.*

axes are found in level 1 at Mugola and in all levels of Kiwore. The proto-Sirewa

*A most inadequate exercise in correlation and interpretation.*

also appear to have been adopting some of the domesticated animals used by

the proto-Chifala. They were however generally much more isolated and the

**? ? ?**

seasonality of the environment caused them to be very late in getting knowledge

of domestication, iron and European materials.

*You have not formulated an hypothesis, only offered an interpretation. Suggest you read Binford to find out the difference.*

In order to test this hypothesis a better description of the pottery should

be produced. No illustrations or detailed descriptions are given. Therefore no

*Hear, hear!*

stylistic similarities can be inferred from the pottery. In the description of Lanu

*A fair comment—but that would be cheating on our part. This kind of irritating uncertainty is not uncommon in the archaeological literature.*

and Kiwore the word "Other" wares is used. Perhaps some of this was similar

to the grey ware found west of the Garna mountains. An attempt should be

*Yes—we need comparable S. Zaronian sequences.*

made to find the origin of the black and red pottery.

Excavations should be carried out at a rock shelter and a mound site in

*i.e., compare the sequences in 2 contrasting types of site in adjoining localities.*

close proximity. In this way one would be able to study the meeting place of the

Chifala and Sirewa peoples. Perhaps one could infer by what methods techniques,

*How about studies of modern Sirewa and Chifala material culture?*

styles, and progressive ideas were transmitted from one culture to another.

*C?-*

*A rather disorganized first attempt and some careless errors, but the main failing is that you have not set up a space-time framework within which you can a) define phases within each sequence, and b) correlate the sequences. In problems like this always prepare a table (see figure 1.5) to summarize the data. This both makes clear what are the main points of similarity and difference between the regional and local sequences and directs your attention to questions/discrepancies requiring a choice between two or more possible explanations.*

*With regard to equations between archaeological and linguistic (or other, for example, oral traditional) sequences: first, develop an interpretation based strictly upon the archaeological evidence, and then and only then compare your archaeological structuring of the past with that of the other discipline and look for similarities, possible correlations or significant differences between them.*

## AN INSTRUCTOR'S ANSWER WITH COMMENTS

### INSTRUCTOR'S ANSWER

It will be convenient to treat Falasia as divided into three main zones: the Anara basin, the Bunyip basin and the West Coast region.

#### a) The Anara Basin

The earliest evidence in the archaeological record comes from the lowest level of Kiwore, where the chipped stone tools, wild animal bones and absence of evidence for agriculture suggest that the area was inhabited by stone age hunting peoples during the last centuries B.C. (dated by C[14]).

Dating of the introduction of agriculture is uncertain since the level in which the first evidence appears is undated and the level above this has only an unreliable bone collagen date. By extrapolating between the layers dated on the basis of more reliable charcoal samples, it seems reasonable to suggest a date of around A.D. 200 for the earliest agriculture, though this may be in error by a couple of centuries. The early agriculturalists lived in continuously or repeatedly occupied villages, as evidenced by the formation of tell-like mounds. They cultivated millet, carbonized grains of which have been found in their pottery, and were using and presumably making iron tools. Domesticated animals, chiefly cattle and goat, were kept. At the beginning of the agricultural occupation these contributed rather little to the meat component of the diet. By around

### COMMENTS

*Region by region treatment, but West Coast not perhaps the best term.*

*The small arrowheads are strongly indicative of the Later Stone Age.*

*Not unreliable exactly—merely not very useful; presumably a very small sample. There is in fact some argument about the relative reliability of bone apatite and bone collagen dates with the latter looking rather better than the other.*

*I agree that they probably did, but it could be a wild relative of the cultivar.*

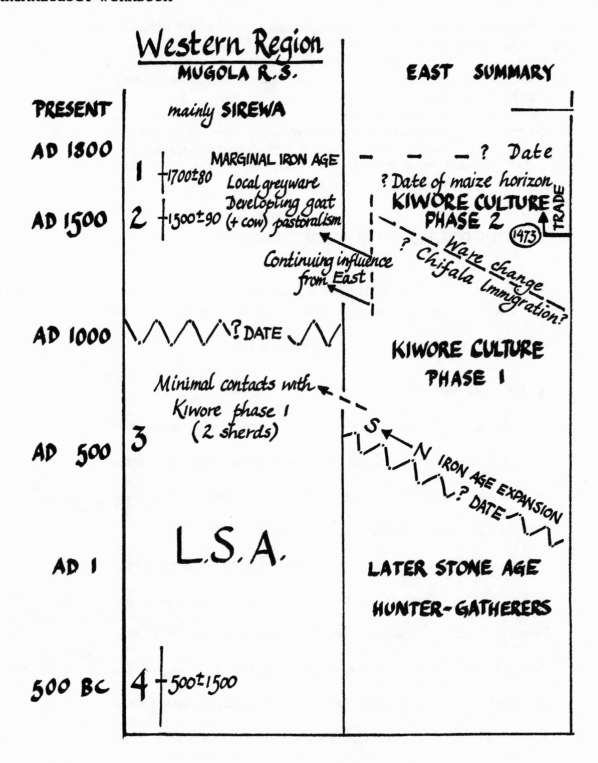

Figure 1.5.  Tabulation of Falasia data

# Eastern Region

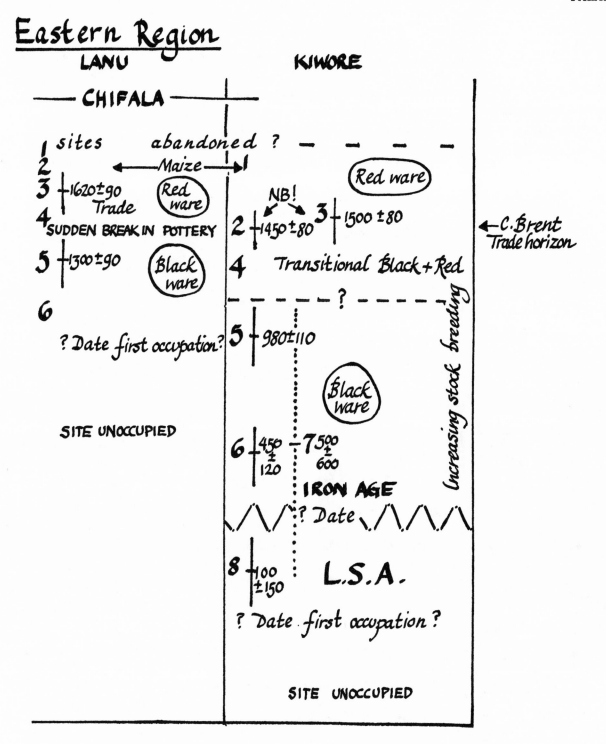

LANU            KIWORE

— CHIFALA —

1   sites    abandoned ? — — — —

2   ←——— Maize ———→

3 ┤1620±90    (Red ware)      (Red ware)

     Trade       NB!

4 SUDDEN BREAK IN POTTERY   2 ┤1450±80   3 ┤1500±80     ←C. Brent

                                 Trade horizon

5 ┤1300±90   (Black ware)   4   Transitional Black + Red

6                  — — — — ? — — — —

   ? Date first occupation?   5 ┤980±110

SITE UNOCCUPIED        (Black ware)     Increasing stock breeding

6 ┤450±120   7 ┤500±600

**IRON AGE**

? Date

8 ┤100±150   **L.S.A.**

? Date first occupation?

SITE UNOCCUPIED

*Not necessarily—the figures refer to bones, and if all the wild animals were elephants. . . . !*

1000 A.D. the importance of wild animals for meat had gradually declined, although hunting continued to provide some 10% of the meat supplies. Black Ware was made by these first farmers.

Since a) pottery of a similar type is known from many sites, b) the economy is reasonably clear, and c) settlement sites are of the same general kind, there is enough evidence to speak of the *Kiwore Culture* (named after the type site) as a historical entity. Further, since all elements of the new economy appear together and no traces of surviving stone age traditions are found in the Kiwore Culture, it seems highly probable that the makers of the culture were immigrants who displaced the indigenous stone age hunters.

*How significant are the 4% B.W. sherds in level 5 and the 2% in 3 (& the 1% in 1)? Poor excavation or unintentional recycling by the prehistoric population could perhaps account for them.*

Beginning about 1000 B.C. and ending by around 1500 A.D. the Black Ware of the Kiwore culture is replaced by a quite different Red Ware. This might be interpreted as a fashion change in the preferred type of pottery, but

*If you are thinking in terms of a major new immigration, this seems very dubious on the archaeological evidence. After all only the pottery seems to change. Settlement type and pattern remain very similar, so does economy. Oral traditions—especially as regards absolute dating further back than about the mid-18th century (in most cases)—are to be accepted only with strong and independent supporting evidence. If on the other hand you are thinking of the immigration of only relatively few but disproportionately influential people, you have a case. I'd like to know more about the oral trads, and also what Brent meant by "king"; might the putative immigrants have introduced a new form of political organization?*

is more probably to be attributed to the gradual infiltration of newcomers entering the area from the north. The area is currently inhabited by Chifala-speaking peoples whose traditions suggest an immigration from the Republic of Zaronia some 800 years ago, and the appearance of the Red Ware occurs at about the same date. It seems most likely therefore that the Red Ware was made by immigrant Chifala people.

There is documentary evidence (Brent's Journal) for European contact at the mouth of the Anara in 1473, and in levels of the Kiwore site which from the radiocarbon dates may reasonably postdate this contact, are found the first imported bronze and glass artifacts. (The inversion of the dates between levels 2 and 3 at Kiwore is trivial since they are less than one standard error apart.) Trade must have continued beyond the first contact, with bronze and glass being traded in and ivory (Brent's Journal) traded out. To this contact also must be attributed the introduction of maize, first evidenced from maize-cob impressions in level 1 at Kiwore.

*Not to Brent in 1473!!, but presumably either to subsequent direct contacts or to diffusion from other African peoples in contact with the Portuguese and others on the coast.*

?

*Are we still in the Kiwore culture? It's pretty dangerous to talk of Chifala culture as far back as the early 2nd millennium A.D. When did the tribal identity evolve?*

b) The Bunyip Basin

No evidence of stone age occupation has yet come to light in the Bunyip basin, but it is likely that further research will reveal this. The preliminary evidence from Lanu, and the distribution of settlement mounds producing Black Ware in the area, show that the Kiwore Culture extended over the Bunyip basin as well as over that of the Anara, though there is as yet no evidence as to whether it started later on the Bunyip.

*Agreed—we need a larger sample of sites and dates*

As in the Anara basin, the Kiwore Culture is replaced by the Red Ware of the Chifala, but on the Bunyip this replacement is considerably later, since the earliest Red Ware is associated with bronze objects and must therefore postdate the European contact. The change from Black Ware to Red Ware between levels 5 and 6 at Lanu is abrupt suggesting the possibility of a short conquest rather than a slow infiltration. If this Chifala conquest is to be dated to about 1500 A.D., a conflict arises with the Chifala oral tradition which speaks of settlement south of the Bunyip 800 years ago. The simplest explanation of this conflict is that in the oral tradition two separate movements have been confused: a first movement from Zaronia to the Anara basin which took place some 800 years ago, and a second movement (the expansion into the Bunyip basin) only 400 years ago. After the Chifala expansion into the Bunyip, imported bronze and glass at Lanu show that external trade was reaching this area, though whether the trade route ran from the mouth of the Anara across the watershed, or whether a second trade route ran upriver from the mouth of the Bunyip is not yet clear. The expansion of Chifala power might perhaps be

*Your previous suggestion has now matured into a fact of history.*

*or appears to be so on the evidence of one site.*

*But there is no other evidence of conquest as far as we know. No destruction level and no major changes in life ways.*

*"Simplest"—well?? Archaeologists have to be very careful about juggling the data and conclusions from other fields without full knowledge of the data or understanding of the methods of analysis and interpretation. This looks like special pleading to me. You add a migration just as Cuvier's pupils multiplied catastrophes to account for the fossil record of extinctions.*

*Given the distribution of sites, which you do not discuss, a trading or exchange network rather than a route is perhaps more likely.*

*Off into speculation again!*

related to their increased wealth obtained from the external trade and their control over it.

### c) The West Coast Region

This includes all the country west of the Garna mountains, and the archaeological record here is much less clear. Stone Age hunters are evidenced at Mugola rock shelter as early as about 500 B.C., and at some time subsequent to this a limited amount of contact with Kiwore Culture people east of the mountains is suggested by the appearance of a little Black Ware in level 3 at Mugola. The occurrence of ground stone axes in this level is unlikely to be related to the practice of agriculture since such axes are commonly used by purely hunting peoples, and the West Coast, with its low rainfall and seasonal rivers would have been an unfavorable region for early agriculture.

The earliest evidence for domestication of animals (Mugola, level 2) dates from about 1500 A.D. and is limited to evidence of domestic goat, as might be expected in a country rather too dry for cattle-keeping. At about the same time, a new type of pottery—the grey pottery—makes its appearance. Two interpretations seem possible: either the stone age hunters had learned the art of pottery-making and domestication of animals from their contacts with the agriculturalists east of the mountains and were now starting to make a distinctive ware of their own, or the remains in level 2 show the beginnings of a movement of new peoples from Zaronia who made the grey pottery and practiced pastoralism. In either case the occurrence of black pottery in the same level requires no particular explanation, because although Chifala settlement of the *lower* Anara basin was complete by this date, we do not know whether the *upper* part of the basin was still inhabited by Kiwore Culture people. We shall not have evidence on

*Not please a verb.*

*Herding and breeding domesticated animals.*

*Is it? Was it? What about the Saharan pastoralists of the 6th and later millennia B.C., or modern Mauretanians, or later pastoralists in western Falasia itself?*

*likely*

*This seems much less likely on the basis of available evidence.*

these points until archaeological work is carried out in southern Zaronia.

By about 1700 A.D. pastoralism was evidently fully established at Mugola and the grey pottery has almost entirely replaced the Black Ware. What few sherds of the latter there are might possibly be connected with refugee Kiwore Culture groups in the Garna mountains or the archaeologically unexplored territory to the east; but this remains speculation in the absence of further evidence. The single imported bead shows that the effects of external trade had penetrated this far, however slightly, whether by contact across the mountains or with traders on the West Coast itself.

*Yes. A potsherd does not make a refugee.*

The ancestors of the Sirewa were presumably the makers of the grey pottery which first appears 200 years before the earliest events referred to in Sirewa oral tradition. Whether the Sirewa are in fact "autochthonous" depends on the interpretation to be put on the evidence from level 2 at Mugola. They might have been immigrant pastoralists from the north, or they may be descended from stone age hunting groups in the West Coast region. If the latter is the case, it is possible that all of Falasia was inhabited by the ancestors of the Sirewa before the introduction of agriculture by the Kiwore Culture people.

*And other culturally related peoples.*

If the glottochronological evidence is to be relied on, and the separation of the Chifala and Sirewa languages dated about 4,000 years ago, this separation must be related to population movements taking place about 2000 B.C., possibly in what is now Zaronia, and belonging to a period earlier than that covered by the present archaeological record.

*It's not, but at best a gross estimate subject to the effects of sociolinguistic and other variables, the workings of which are still not satisfactorily understood.*

*Obviously you have been trained in the British tradition (an American-trained archaeologist would have been more formal in his definition of phases, etc.), and you were rushed when you prepared this for your class. I am surprised that you didn't consider the significance of the differences in the number of sites that have given Black and Red Wares and in their distributions, including the interesting absence of Red Ware sites in the upper Bunyip basin. Is there anything special about the Chifala there? And although Brent's mention of a "king" must, like all historical sources, be considered in the context of its time, it does raise interesting questions about the early Chifala (in your terminology) or Kiwore Culture, phase 2 (in mine) political system. Why, by the way, did you not make use of the excellent* Ethnography of Falasia *for descriptions of traditional Chifala and Sirewa material culture and life ways?*

# The Hacienda Plain

The Hacienda Plain, on the Pacific coast of Central America, is bounded on the west by the ocean and on the east by the Zatopec Highlands (fig. 2.1). The climate is tropical and the annual rainfall about 90 inches, the vegetation being dense jungle. There has been little modern development, and the Nanosec Indians, the inhabitants of the plain, live for the most part in small, scattered farming communities. The Zatopec Highlands rise steeply to over 3,000 feet, have an annual rainfall of about 35 inches, and are mostly open grassland. In the highlands there are modern cities, and the Zatopec Indians have been integrated into the industrial economy.

The highlands are rich in mineral ores, particularly gold, but no metal resources are known from the Hacienda Plain.

Linguistic analysis of the modern Nanosec and Zatopec languages, supplemented by word lists found in the writings of early Spanish colonists, suggests that the languages are of the same family but that they separated from each other a considerable time ago, perhaps two to three thousand years.

The following is an excerpt from the journal of Felipe Huile de Givado, a Spanish explorer writing in the year 1670:

> One hundred and fifty years after Cortes first planted the flag of Spain in the Americas, after passing through the high country where live the Zatopecs and marveling at their stone-built temples, I descended into the hot, humid forest of the plain to which I gave the name "Hacienda." There dwell a poor people called the Nanosecs who live in hamlets and gain a bare subsistence from their primitive farming. Near one of their villages I stumbled upon a platform or small earthen pyramid, only 10 feet high, which served as a place of worship for some dozen hamlets. Some two days later, to my great amazement, I encountered a huge stone pyramid, overgrown with vines and creepers and so tall that it reached up even above the tops of the trees.

In recent years there has been little archaeological work in the Zatopec Highlands, but during the 1930s several expeditions from the University of Pyewacket examined the Zatopec stone-built temples and recovered a number of inscriptions in an early dialect of Zatopec. These inscriptions contain references to the "Totalrecs who live between the mountains and the great sea where the sun sets." They speak of raiding parties, led by named Totalrec rulers, making surprise attacks on Zatopec centers before retiring into the

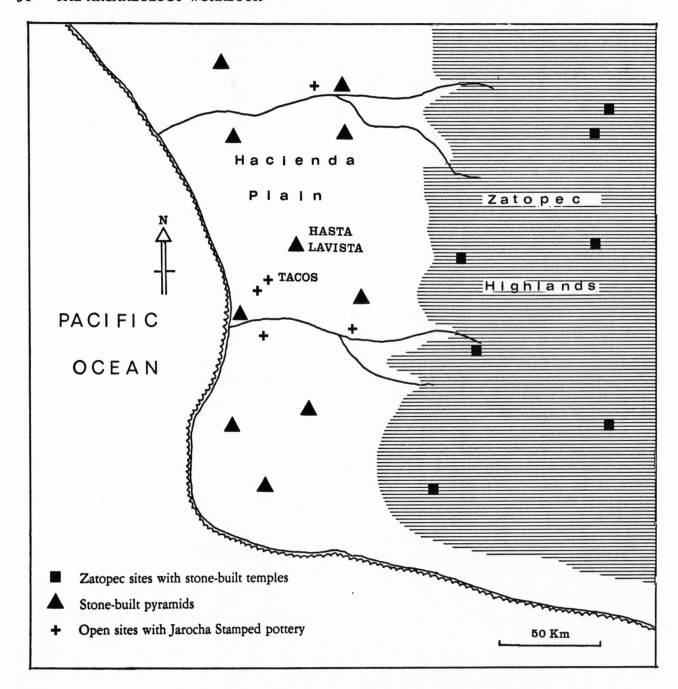

**Figure 2.1.** Map showing the Hacienda Plain and the Zatopec Highlands

jungle with their plunder of precious ornaments and other goods. Linguistically it is clear that the names of the Totalrec rulers belong to a language unrelated to Zatopec.

Serious archaeological work on the Hacienda Plain began only ten years ago and has been hampered by the dense jungle and lack of roads. Air photography has produced some results, and a small amount of reconnaissance has been carried out on foot. There have been two excavations, one at the pyramid complex of Hasta Lavista, the other at an open village site called Tacos. Some of the results of these excavations are given below.

The excavations at Tacos were extensive, particularly the West Trench, which produced large quantities of potsherds (table 2.1). No traces of stone buildings were found at the site.

**Tacos**

In addition to the pottery, a number of stone axes and hoes were found at all levels, as well as cassava graters and carbonized seeds of gourds. A single terracotta jaguar figurine was found in Level 3. It is similar in style to others from Hasta Lavista. The Nova Embossed pottery can be paralleled by many pieces from the Pyramid of the Sun at the same site.

**TABLE 2.1. Tacos, West Trench: percentage frequencies of pottery types and radiocarbon dates by level**

| Level | Jarocha Stamped | Nova Embossed | Other | C$^{14}$ Dates |
|---|---|---|---|---|
| 1 | 82 | — | 18 | |
| 2 | 84 | 3 | 13 | A.D. 1490 $\pm$ 50 |
| 3 | 80 | 5 | 15 | |
| 4 | 79 | 6 | 15 | |
| 5 | 92 | — | 8 | A.D. 960 $\pm$ 100 |
| 6 | 88 | — | 12 | A.D. 875 $\pm$ 90 |

Jarocha Stamped—coiled pottery made of a montmorillonitic clay containing iron compounds and fired for a short period in an oxidizing atmosphere
Nova Embossed—mold-made pottery in a carbonaceous kaolinitic clay fired under carefully controlled reducing conditions

The Pyramid of the Sun at **Hasta Lavista** is constructed of carefully shaped and faced stone blocks and has a stairway. It is richly decorated with bas-reliefs of jaguar heads, their teeth bared in a distinctive grin. Pyramid X2 is a small stepped pyramid made of rammed earth and without surviving ornamentation.

**Hasta Lavista (figure 2.2)**

Level A contained large amounts of well-fired and elaborately decorated black pottery, as well as a few sherds of a poor quality red ware similar to that from Tacos. There were also a number of figurines representing jaguars with bared teeth. The pottery from Level B consists almost entirely of red ware, although a few black sherds occur at the very top of the level. Charcoal from a hearth at the base of Level B gave a date of A.D. 720 $\pm$ 150.

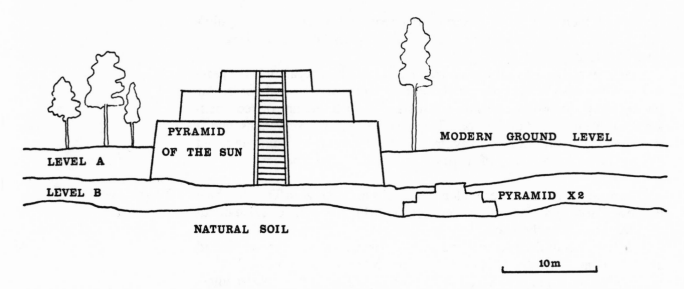

**Figure 2.2.**    Hasta Lavista: rough sketch showing the relationship of the Pyramid of the Sun to Pyramid X2

What can be said on the basis of this evidence of the prehistory of the Hacienda Plain? You are advised to begin your analysis by constructing a table summarizing the data.

# The Island of Coolay

## PROBLEM 3

It looks as though archaeological jobs are going to be as hard to come by in the 1990s as they were in the eighties. You had found temporary work on a salvage project in the Yukon when you heard of a position on the North Atlantic island of Coolay. Knowing nothing of the island, you fired off an application and today, 15 April 1990, received the letter reproduced on the following page. Unfortunately you have no libraries or other resources available, and they need your answer *A.S.A.P.* As their letter indicates, notes on the geography, history, and archaeology of the island have been included in order to help you prepare your answer, and these are reproduced below.

### Notes on
### Our Island Story

by

S. C. H.

Coolay is a large island in the North Atlantic Ocean, measuring about 320 kilometers from north to south (fig. 3.1). Lya Ness, at its southeastern tip, lies 449 kilometers due west of Dunmore Head in Ireland. The northwest of the island is mountainous, with peaks towering to over 800 meters, while the southeast is low-lying and gently undulating country. Thanks to its oceanic situation, the climate is equable, except in the mountains, although strong gales are frequent in winter. The vegetation is mainly grassland, with extensive peat bogs. Trees are almost entirely lacking, save for small woods on sheltered parts of the southwest coast around Llanbrendan.

The modern population, sparse by European standards, is a unique blend of Celtic, Roman, and Scandinavian stocks. Over the past two centuries, political considerations have resulted in strong cultural ties with Scandinavia, and archaeological work has concentrated on the Viking invasion and later periods. Recently, however, there have been bitter disputes over fishing rights in waters off Iceland and Greenland, and sentiment has turned away from the Scandinavian connection. A drastic fall in the tonnage of fish landed has led to a search for alternative economic strategies, since sheep rearing, the Island's only other major source of foreign exchange, is, on its own, insufficient. Coolay has, on the other hand, derived some financial benefit from its strategic position and has allowed the establishment of a foreign military air base at Penmerryn on the northwest coast. There is an ambitious program to

## Early Heritage Research and Monitoring Commission
### P.O. Box 472
### Erikshavn, Coolay

1 April 1990

Director of Archaeological Research

Dear Candidate,

I have to inform you that the Commission is most appreciative of your interest in the above position and that your name has been included amongst those short-listed candidates being invited to come to the Island for interview.

I am further directed to bring to your attention the following extract from the Early Heritage (1990) Bill, which was enacted by the Populum Thing on 25 March and now has the force of law.

Section 246a Archaeological research
*The Archaeological Section of the E.H.R.M.C. shall have the following as its primary research aims:*

1. Discovery of the earliest human settlement on the Island.
2. Reconstruction of the original vegetation pattern and of its subsequent modification by man and weather.
3. Reconstruction of pre-Romano-Coolish national/tribal territories.
4. Discovery of the nature and extent of Romano-Coolish penetration of the highland zone.
5. Location and thorough investigation of as many pre-Viking archaeological sites as possible.

It is the desire of the Commissioners that, in anticipation of the interview and at your earliest convenience, you submit a plan of research in which you *comment on these aims, assign priorities,* and *describe how you would attempt,* if appointed, *to fulfill them while resolving any conflicts between the aims that might conceivably arise.*

I have pleasure in conveying you the attached notes on the geography, history and archaeology of the Island of Coolay. These may be of some assistance in the preparation of your research plan.

Yours sincerely,

Siobhain Candidus Hairybreeks
Secretary to the Commission

Encls.

convert much of the lowlands from grazing to arable and to develop a large hydroelectric scheme on the upper Jotunsa River and extensive electronic and light industry plants around Erikshavn and New Menor. It is the change in national sentiment, coupled with the impending plowing of much of lowland Coolay, that has led to the setting up of the Early Heritage Research and Monitoring Commission, whose terms of reference are to preserve as much as possible of our pre-Viking heritage.

Written information on the pre-Viking periods is confined to Romano-Coolish inscriptions and the Last Lay of Tigdradasdottir, which chronicles the final Viking victory and its aftermath.

The Romano-Coolish period began in the third century B.C., when a Roman merchant vessel was blown off course as a result of damage sustained in a small engagement during the Second Punic War. Swept through the Pillars of Hercules, the ship was finally beached at the mouth of the river Vinalven, where an initial settlement, Castrum Fortunatum, was founded at the site of the modern Caistor. Fabulus Altus, the ship's captain, quickly achieved prominence among the local people; the Romans took Coolish wives and made no attempt to return to their former homes. Roman ideas and influence spread throughout the Coolay lowlands, and Fabulus' descendants became absolute monarchs under the title *Gubernator.* Their kingdom, known as Thule, seems to have been generally peaceful, though deaths in border skirmishes with the inhabitants of the mountains are recorded in the *Corpus Inscriptorum.* It is believed that the culture of Thule stemmed not from Roman conquest, but rather from the fusion of Roman and native Celtic cultural elements. There seems to have been little or no contact with Roman Europe, though early references to vineyards in the Vinalven Valley have been cited as evidence of such. However this may be, the language of the inscriptions gradually changes over the Romano-Coolish period, becoming less and less like the original Latin.

Around A.D. 200 there was an incursion of peoples from the highland zone; fortified Romano-Coolish camps were sacked, and a new form of government, the *Concilius Populom,* emerged. The extent of this council's authority is uncertain. Nor is it clear how much it represented the highland Celts rather than the Romano-Coolish alone. In the ninth century, the *Concilius* found itself unable to ensure the defense of the island in the face of early Viking raids. Delegation of full military authority to an officer known as the *Dus Bonom* proved ineffective, and in A.D. 962, the Romano-Coolish army was defeated at the Battle of Erikshavn, site of the present capital. Coolay became, in effect, a Viking colony but with the cultures of its previous inhabitants submerged rather than eradicated.

The archaeology of the Viking period is well known. Figure 3.1 shows the locations of the pre-Viking sites identified to date. Since there has been little archaeological activity concerned with these periods, there are likely to be many more sites. In the early 1900s, the Society for Thulian Studies carried out a brief but intensive program of excavations on Romano-Coolish sites, whence came the inscriptions. Six villas in the southeast and four fortified camps were investigated. The excavations were meticulously published, and the finds are still safely warehoused in Caistor, but the work was addressed primarily to chronology and architectural studies and contains no usable information on land use or economy. The camp at Caistor was set up in the third century B.C. and those along the edge of the highlands in the

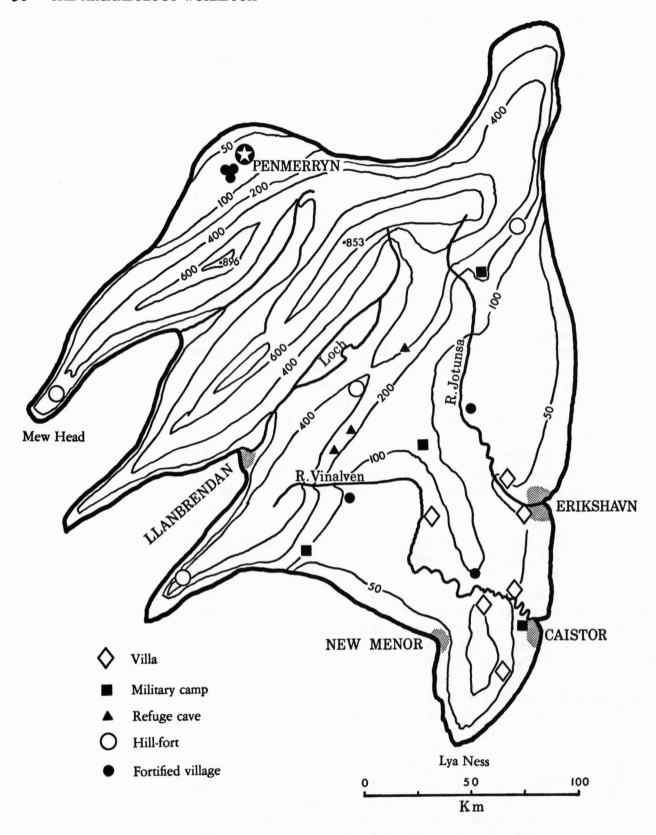

**Figure 3.1.** Modern settlements and pre-Viking sites on the island of Coolay (contour heights in meters)

first century A.D. There is, however, no exact chronology, since despite the dating of many inscriptions *ab Urbe condita* (from the foundation of Rome), it is clear that this count became unreliable on more than one occasion.

A Romano-Coolish pottery sequence was worked out, and the chronology is based on this as much as on the inscriptions. From the third century B.C. to the second century A.D., a wheel-made painted ware is overwhelmingly dominant. Varieties of the types defined are considered to be datable to within about 40 years. In the third century, handmade pottery becomes more common and is found associated with a degenerate form of the painted ware. From the middle of the fourth century until the Viking conquest, mold-made pottery enters the record, but neither its varieties nor those of the handmade ceramics can be securely dated.

No pre-Roman sites have been excavated in the southeast, but in the northwest, salvage work during the construction of Penmerryn Air Base uncovered three sites interpreted as fortified villages. At each one, from ten to twenty hut circles delimited by post holes were surrounded by a low earthwork, some forty meters in diameter, which may have carried a stockade. From one of these came the only available radiocarbon date of 3500 $\pm$ 170 B.P. Similar circular earthworks have been identified at three locations in the southeastern lowlands. In the highland zone four hill-forts are reported. These occupy commanding positions and are surrounded by concentric walls of earth, or, in the case of the site on Mew Head, of dry, uncoursed stone.

The only other known sites are three caves on the eastern edge of the highland zone. They are believed to contain deep deposits. Surface collections include both late Romano-Coolish potsherds and various Viking artifacts, suggesting that they were used as refuges during the conquest.

# The Kara Kavan

The Kara Kavan is a region in Central Asia, in the border area between India (to the south), the USSR (to the north and west), and the People's Republic of China (to the east). The Kara Kavan is bounded by three ranges of high and almost impassable mountains: the Sek Kong Shan in the north, the Fan Ling Shan to the south, and the Sha Tin Shan to the east. Between each pair of mountain ranges, there is a pass, so that there are three ways of entering the Kara Kavan (figure 4.1).

Rainfall in the Kara Kavan is low and seasonal. Most of the area is semidesert, supporting a seasonal crop of grass after the rains but reverting to desert conditions in the dry season. A number of small oases provide water for humans and desert animals. The only environmentally distinct area is the valley of the Hsien Ho, which flows eastward across the region before passing between the Fan Ling Shan and the Sha Tin Shan into China. The Hsien Ho Valley provides a narrow belt of fertile and well-watered country. Today the main products of the Kara Kavan are vegetables, grown under intensive irrigation in the Hsien Ho Valley, and Astrakhan, the wool of the Karakul sheep, which graze freely on the grass of the semidesert when this is available, but are rounded up and brought down into the Hsien Ho Valley during the dry season.

Due to its position between the separate agricultural and urban areas of Southwest Asia and China, the Kara Kavan has long been subjected to influences from both East and West and is a key area for understanding the relationships between them. Another factor that may have affected the history of the Kara Kavan is the area to the north of the Sek Kong Shan, where mounted nomadism was fully established by about 500 B.C.

In historic times the area saw repeated population movements, and no oral tradition survives to throw light on the older archaeological finds. However, two references from ancient historical sources appear to refer to events in the Kara Kavan. Excerpts from these are given below; the first is from a contemporary Chinese documentary by an unknown author:

> For the previous twenty years the Ta Tai Wan had been a serious threat to the safety of the Western Provinces. These Ta Tai Wan were horse-riding barbarians, many of them with white skins, blue eyes and yellow hair. They knew little of civilization and their chief delight was in fighting and plunder. At first they were content with gifts, but soon they could not contain their

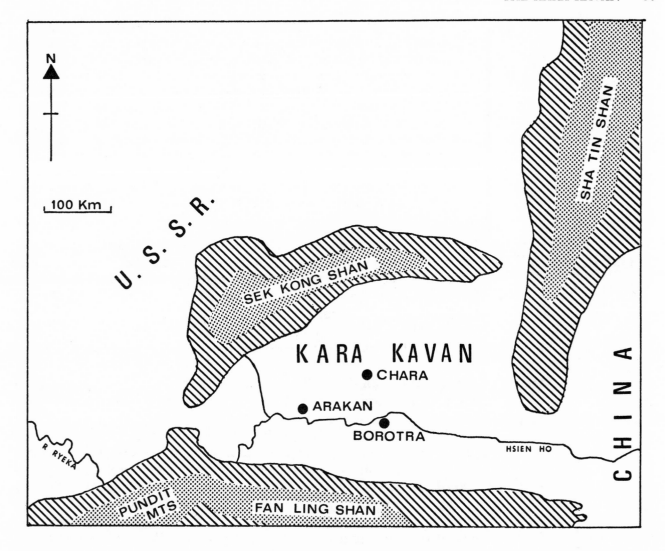

**Figure 4.1.** Part of Central Asia

greed and raided far and wide in the Western Provinces and the Viceroy of the Western Provinces could not restrain them. Accordingly in this year [129 B.C.], the Emperor sent General Wu with a large force into the homeland of the Ta Tai Wan. He marched between the mountains into the valley of the headwaters of the Hsien Ho and there utterly defeated the Ta Tai Wan, capturing three of their bear's-tail standards, so that they fled from the land and were seen no more. Then General Wu established a garrison at Bien To on the Hsien Ho and there was peace for many years on the Western Frontier, and the whole of the valley of the Hsien Ho was added to the Emperor's dominions.

The second piece of information comes from "The Parthian Annals," a little-known work by the Roman author Felonius Fibula, written in the first century A.D., and treating the history of Parthia, a kingdom that was a constant enemy of Rome and was situated in the area now occupied by the modern country of Iran. The events described in this extract refer to the period 125–115 B.C.:

Not only did Mithridates have to fight against the enemy on the western front of his kingdom, but also in the north-east the province of Margiana was invaded by the barbarian Ourophores, which being translated means "the tail-bearers." These were a fierce people who rode on horses and traveled with all their women, their children and their cows. According to Parthian writers, they had issued from the mountain passes far to the east beyond the headwaters of the River Sarassus [the modern River Ryeka]. They were terrible to behold, with their yellow skins and narrow eyes: they knew neither crops nor cities and men said that they had been sent from the underworld by Ahriman himself, but of the truth of this I cannot speak. However, after three years of hard campaigning, Mithridates broke their power and restored the province of Margiana to the Kingdom of Parthia.

**ARCHAEO-LOGICAL DATA:** Intensive archaeological research has been carried out in the Kara Kavan for the last ten years, with aerial photography and considerable reconnaissance work using special desert vehicles. Preliminary accounts of three excavations have been released. No detailed sections have been published, but the excavations have given a number of radiocarbon dates. The distributions of various artifact types have also been mapped (figure 4.2).

The following is a summary of the reports on the three excavated sites:

**1. Arakan** Arakan is an open site in the upper valley of the Hsien Ho. Three distinct levels were recognized at the site and are ascribed by the excavators to three periods.

Level 1. This, the uppermost level, has a radiocarbon date from near the base of $2400 \pm 100$ B.P. The most striking find in this level was a large pit burial containing the body of a chieftain accompanied by twelve of his retainers and four horses. Amongst the rich grave goods were bronze ritual vessels of Chinese manufacture, gold and bronze dress ornaments, pieces of bronze horse harness, and a bronze staff or standard at the top of which is a ring. Numerous sherds of plain black pottery were found, but there was no evidence of permanent housing.

Level 2. In this level were found the foundations of at least four mud-built rectangular houses, each measuring some $10 \times 10$ meters. Carbonized seeds of wheat and barley were found together with clay-lined pits, which may have been used for storing grain. Bones of domestic sheep and goat were also present. A copper dagger was found near the top of this level, but most of the tools are made of stone, either chipped or ground, as in the case of the ground stone axes with their characteristic "D"-shaped cross section. The pottery is well fired and decorated with black-and-red painted spirals. The excavators have compared this pottery to that from the Pundit culture, known to have flourished in the northern foothills of the Pundit Mountains between 5000 and 4000 B.P. A radiocarbon date for the middle of this level gave an estimate of $4250 \pm 125$ B.P. Two human skeletons are reported to be of "European" racial type.

Level 3. This level contained numerous chipped stone tools and bone artifacts such as harpoons and needles. There were bones of wild horse and several species of deer. No pottery was found, nor any traces of structures. There are two radiocarbon dates from this level, an upper one of $7500 \pm 190$ B.P. and a lower one of $10,340 \pm 200$ B.P.

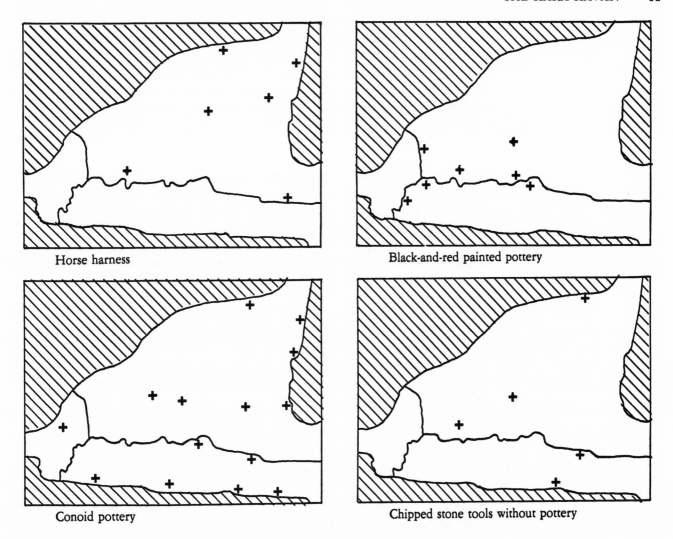

Horse harness

Black-and-red painted pottery

Conoid pottery

Chipped stone tools without pottery

**Figure 4.2.**   Find-places of various kinds of artifact in the Kara Kavan

**Borotra** takes its name from the nearby modern village. Excavation at the site was initiated after aerial photography had shown the presence of a large rectangular structure, subdivided internally into smaller rectangular units. Excavation revealed that the structure had an outer defensive wall built of stone. Some plain black pottery was found, not unlike that from Level 1 at Arakan. Iron and bronze spears, iron crossbow mechanisms, and ritual bronze vessels are all clearly of Han Dynasty Chinese manufacture. Stylistic details of the bronze vessels place them in the early part of that dynasty between 202 and *c.* 150 B.C. A charcoal sample from an inner room gave a date of 2200 ± 100 B.P.

    Stratified below the remains of this structure were those of a small village settlement with mud-built house foundations and black-and-red painted pottery similar to that from Level 2 at Arakan. Tools include ground stone axes with "D"-shaped cross section, many chipped stone tools and (towards the top of the level) several copper daggers and a copper axe. There was a radiocarbon date of 3700 ± 150 B.P. from the base of this level.

**2. Borotra**

In the third and lowest layer were sherds of a different kind of pottery, decorated with cord impressions and conoid in shape, being generally similar to the earliest pottery found in Japan, China, and Southeast Asia. Animal bones included those of deer, wild pig, and water fowl. Bone harpoons and chipped stone tools were found, as well as ground stone axes of rectangular cross section. A single human skeleton is reported to be of Mongoloid racial type.

**3. Chara**    Chara lies about halfway between the Hsien Ho and the Sek Kong Shan, in the central Kara Kavan. It is situated at a small oasis that provides year-round water. Three levels were distinguished, Level A being the latest.

Level A. No structures were recognized in this level, but a number of sherds of plain black pottery were found, together with pieces of bronze horse harness. From the top of the level, but clearly associated with it, came an iron crossbow mechanism of Han Dynasty type. Charcoal was not collected.

Level B. Again no structures were seen. Pottery was almost entirely conoid in shape and decorated with cord impressions, though three sherds of black-and-red painted ware were found in the upper part. Two radiocarbon dates for this level are 6100 $\pm$ 200 B.P. and 3600 $\pm$ 170 B.P. for the lower and upper parts, respectively.

Level C. Chipped stone tools and a bone harpoon were recovered. Also present were bones of deer, wild horse, and various small desert rodents. This level was dated to 8620 $\pm$ 220 B.P.

How much can be inferred from the above about past human activity in the Kara Kavan? Can you detect changes in the economic basis? What can be said about the relationship through time between the Kara Kavan and neighboring areas? Does the archaeological record contain traces of the Ta Tai Wan or of the Ourophores?

# Petristan

The state of Petristan in the Indian subcontinent lies across the watershed between the upper reaches of the Paratha River system to the west and the Korma River to the east (figure 5.1). The state extends northwards into the foothills of the great mountains of Parasmaipada where narrow and remote valleys stretch north toward the continental divide. Southern Petristan is gentler country, today supporting flourishing cereal agriculture. To the south of the state, lower than the Parasmaipada but still a formidable range, rise the Rasgullas, and south again is the great desert of the Sandesh. Throughout recorded history, southern Petristan has had considerable commercial and strategic importance as the main route between the Korma and Paratha basins.

The early civilization of the Paratha Valley has long been recognized as one of the past glories of southern Asia. It flourished from about 2700 to 1700 B.C. and is represented at many sites in the Paratha basin. A number of village sites are known, but it is the urban centers that have attracted most attention, and none more than the great city of Talawa Magazh, believed to have been the commercial and administrative capital. While the script has been deciphered, the ancient Paratha Valley language is still poorly understood, since long texts are exceedingly rare. Most inscriptions are found on stamp seals that always bear only one or two words with genitival endings, presumably personal names indicating possession. Prior to about 2200 B.C., the seals were square ended and carried representations of bulls and goats. After this date, they were mostly rectangular and had only the inscription.

Recent finds have suggested that the extent of Paratha Valley influence may be much wider than previously thought. In particular there is a suggestion that much or all of Petristan formed, in some sense, part of the Paratha Valley sphere of influence. The Petristan State Archaeological Survey has started to investigate this question and has made a large number of surface collections from likely sites. Careful and prolonged work has produced collections consisting in each case of at least 5,000 sherds selected by random sampling techniques. Fifteen of the sites are thought to be single-period villages, and these are indicated on figure 5.1 by a code letter. Two urban sites, Garam Masala and Tiltandula, have also been sampled, while at the city

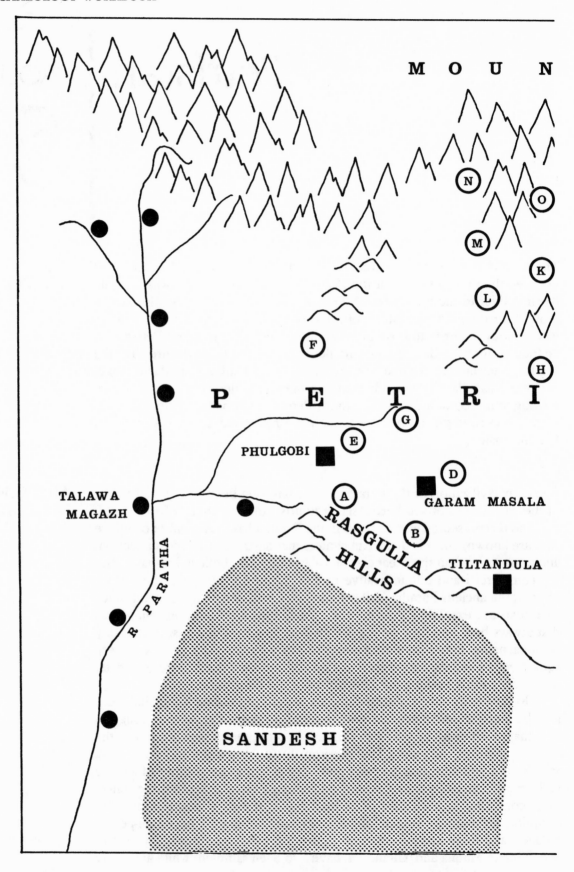

**Figure 5.1.** Early pottery-yielding sites in Petristan and urban sites in the Paratha basin

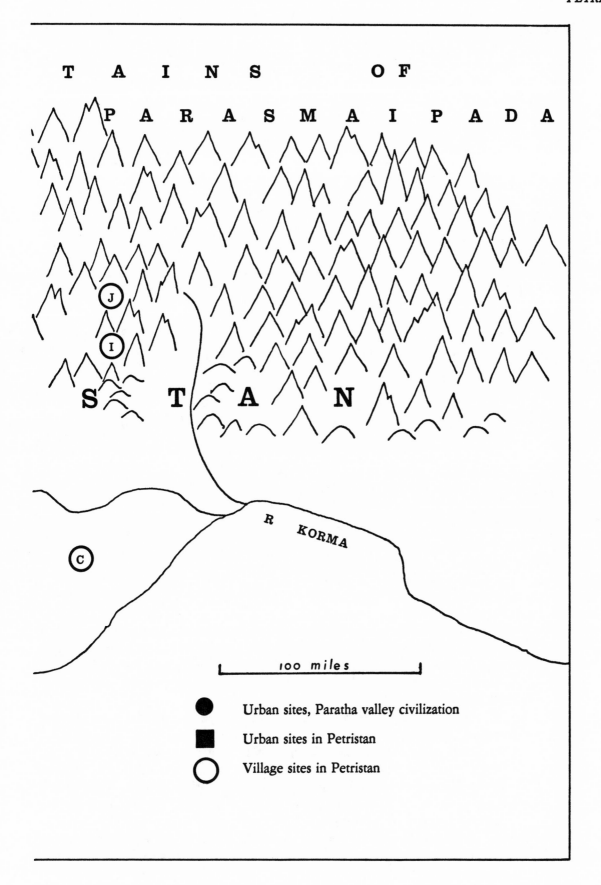

T A I N S        O F

P A R A S M A I P A D A

S       T       A       N

R   KORMA

100 miles

● Urban sites, Paratha valley civilization

■ Urban sites in Petristan

○ Village sites in Petristan

**TABLE 5.1.** Percentages of pottery types and numbers of Paratha Valley seals from Petristan sites

| SITES | W1 | W2 | W3 | F1 | F2 | F3 | F4 | F5 | C | Z | Petristani Monochrome | Sq. | Rect. |
|---|---|---|---|---|---|---|---|---|---|---|---|---|---|
| | | | | | POTTERY TYPES (%) | | | | | | | SEALS | |
| A | 22.8 | | | 1.7 | | | 3.7 | | 30.3 | | 41.5 | | |
| B | 17.6 | 0.6 | | 7.3 | | | | | 21.1 | | 43.5 | 1 | 1 |
| C | 20.3 | | | 0.8 | | | 7.3 | | 27.9 | | 43.7 | | 2 |
| D | 1.4 | 10.4 | | 6.3 | | | | 6.4 | 9.0 | | 66.5 | 1 | |
| E | 21.2 | | | 5.8 | | | 0.6 | | 27.0 | | 45.4 | | 1 |
| F | | 18.1 | | 1.0 | | | | 7.5 | 14.1 | | 59.3 | | |
| G | 6.2 | 7.4 | | 7.1 | | | | 4.4 | 17.2 | | 57.7 | | |
| H | | 15.2 | | 2.8 | | | | 7.7 | 4.1 | | 70.2 | | |
| I | 12.2 | | 12.1 | | 2.5 | 0.9 | | | 14.6 | | 57.7 | | |
| J | 0.9 | | 8.9 | | 13.7 | | | | 4.1 | | 72.5 | | |
| K | 3.1 | | 10.4 | | 10.8 | | | | 7.0 | | 68.7 | | |
| L | 17.4 | | 3.0 | | | 3.4 | | | 22.3 | | 53.9 | | |
| M | | | 7.2 | | 15.2 | | | | 0.2 | | 77.4 | | |
| N | 16.5 | | | | | | 4.7 | | 28.8 | | 50.0 | | |
| O | 15.4 | | 7.6 | | 1.2 | 1.9 | | | 18.0 | | 55.9 | | |
| Garam Masala | 0.6 | 8.4 | | 5.0 | | | | 6.6 | 10.5 | 1.4 | 67.4 | 1 | |
| Tiltandula | 20.3 | | | 0.7 | | | 3.7 | | 23.1 | 4.5 | 47.7 | | 2 |
| Phul-Gobi Upper | 19.3 | | | 4.7 | | | 0.1 | | 26.0 | 4.8 | 45.1 | | 1 |
| Phul-Gobi Lower | 9.8 | 4.0 | | 6.6 | | | | 1.3 | 21.0 | 2.7 | 54.6 | 1 | |

of Phul-gobi, a test pit was dug with the specific intention of recovering a ceramic sequence. Section drawings are not available, but it is reported that only two levels were recognized as stratigraphically distinct. Two radiocarbon dates have been released: 2100 $\pm$ 50 B.C. for the upper level and 2450 $\pm$ 70 B.C. for the lower.

Table 5.1 gives percentages of pottery types from the excavation and surface collections. A high proportion of the sherds from all sites are of Petristani monochrome ware. Types W1 to W3 are water storage pots, while types F1 to F5 are food containers. These are distinctive painted forms and are not closely paralleled in neighboring regions. Type C is a cooking vessel of Paratha Valley type with a very fine slip and burnish that reduces porosity. It is found widely in the Paratha basin in numbers suggesting that it was in general popular use there. Type Z, probably a ceremonial vessel, is also an exotic from the Paratha Valley civilization. It is known to have been produced commercially at Talawa Magazh over a long period and was exported from there to other Paratha Valley sites where it is only found in temples and in the most stately and luxurious pleasure domes. Also shown in table 5.1 are the actual numbers of Paratha Valley seals found in Petristan.

Can you suggest a chronology for the sites and pottery types of Petristan? Is there evidence suggesting that nonchronological factors influence the pottery frequencies?

# The Sierra de la Serenidad Complex

**BACKGROUND INFORMATION:**

The Sierra de la Serenidad complex is the name given by South Americanist archaeologists to the exceptionally well studied groups of settlements in the river basins on either side of the Sierra de la Serenidad, which date to the last quarter of the first millennium A.D. Due to the very large amount of information available, only a selection is presented here, other aspects being summarized or omitted.

The map (figure 6.1) shows the high mountains of the sierra running from north to south and crossed only by one feasible pass near the Lago de Handel, a high altitude lake. To the west of the mountains, the coastal plain, divided into the river basins of the Rio Amontillado and the Rio Oloroso, slopes gradually to the sea. The climate becomes progressively drier from the mountains toward the west, culminating in a desert strip that runs unbroken along the coast. On the eastern part of the coastal plain, climate and soil combine to support a flourishing maize-based agricultural economy, which is generally thought to have existed for the past 2,000 years. There is also evidence that fish constituted a considerable part of the diet of the inhabitants of settlements near the larger rivers. Agriculture was also possible in the region of the Lago de Handel, where today potatoes are extensively grown. To the east of the sierra, grasslands give way to forest, and the staple crop varies with decreasing altitude, changing from maize to manioc (cassava).

**ARCHAEO-LOGICAL DATA:**

The great majority of recorded sites in the area are settlements; other types of sites are not shown on the maps. Settlements can be classified with some confidence into three categories according to their areas, which show a multimodal distribution. The largest cover between 15 and 22 hectares and include extensive use of shaped and faced stone walling. There are three such sites: Criadera, Solera, and Raya. Others vary between five and eight hectares; some, but not all, of these contain small amounts of stone walling. Bodega, near the Lago de Handel, is one such site. The remaining settlement sites have not produced stone walling and are under three hectares in extent.

Four major pottery styles are characteristic of the period in question: Criadera Red in the middle Amontillado basin; Bodega Black-on-buff in the Lago de Handel and Upper Amontillado regions; Solera Painted in the Oloroso basin; and Raya Fluted in the basin of the Rio Manzanilla east of the sierra. There is a strong tendency for the distributions of these styles to be mutually exclusive (see fig. 6.1). Within the areas of these pottery styles, various distinctive vessel forms and other traits have been identified. Figure 6.2 shows the distribution of such characters within the Manzanilla basin; the pattern that appears is broadly representative of those in the other three style areas.

Three obsidian flows have been identified in the upper Amontillado region, and their products can be reliably distinguished by neutron activation analysis. The occurrence of knives made from these obsidians is shown in figure 6.3. Obsidian is not used outside the Amontillado basin, but in the valleys of the Oloroso and Manzanilla, chalcedony knives are found. Figure 6.3 also shows the distribution in the Amontillado basin of pendants made from the shell of the southern pearl mussel, a marine shellfish common along the west coast.

Two classes of object appear to be exotic, and both are believed to be of northern origin. Metalworking is not characteristic of the Sierra de la Serenidad complex, but there have been sporadic finds of bronze knives typologically similar in the shape of the handle and slightly raised central rib to others from the Portorubio area 1,100 kilometers to the north. Northern stylistic influences are also apparent in a small number of jade plaques. One example each has been found at Solera and Criadera and two examples at Raya, although there is no known source of jade in the area. The bronze knives are much more numerous, and figure 6.4 shows their distribution in the Oloroso basin.

Harpoons are common in riverine sites, there being a wide range of forms. As an example, figure 6.5 shows the dominant forms found at excavated sites along the Rio Amontillado del Sur, the southernmost branch of the Amontillado.

Figure 6.6 illustrates some typical artifacts of the Serenidad complex.


What can be said about modes of production and distribution in the Sierra de la Serenidad complex, and to what further inferences might such an analysis, taken in conjunction with the other data, lead?

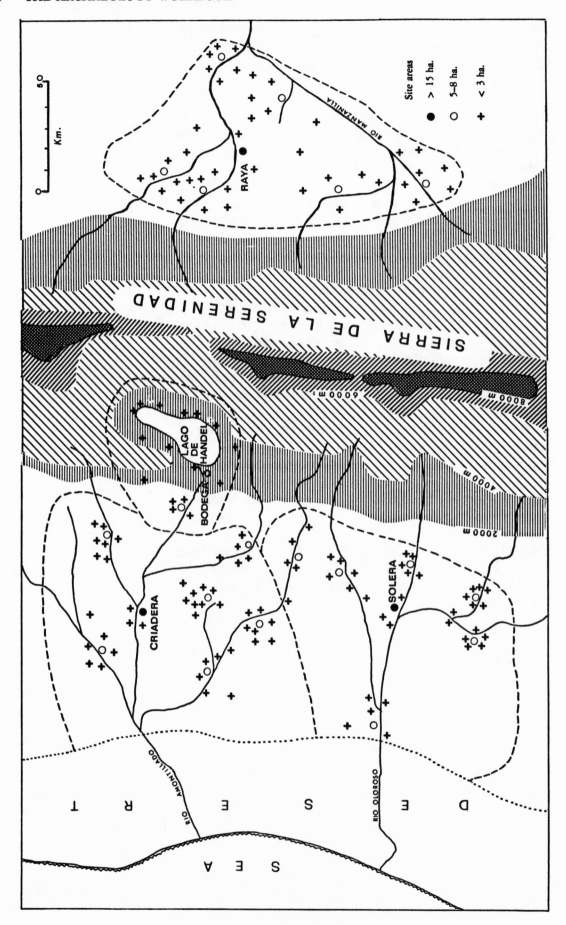

**Figure 6.1.** Sites and distributions of the major pottery styles in the Sierra de la Serenidad

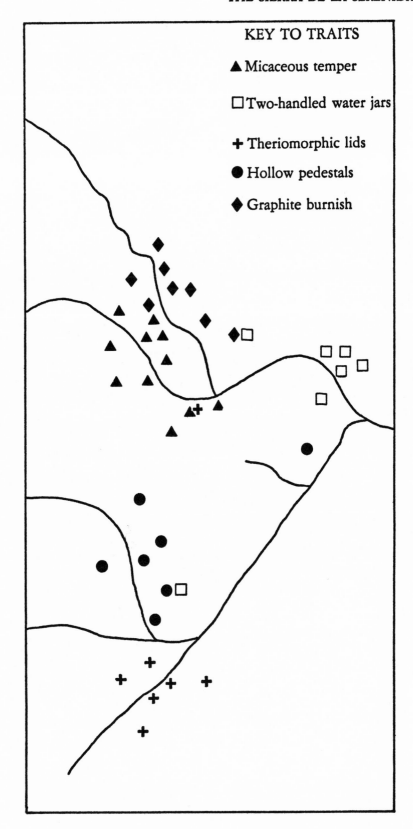

**Figure 6.2.** Occurrences of various traits characteristic of the Raya Fluted style of the Manzanilla basin

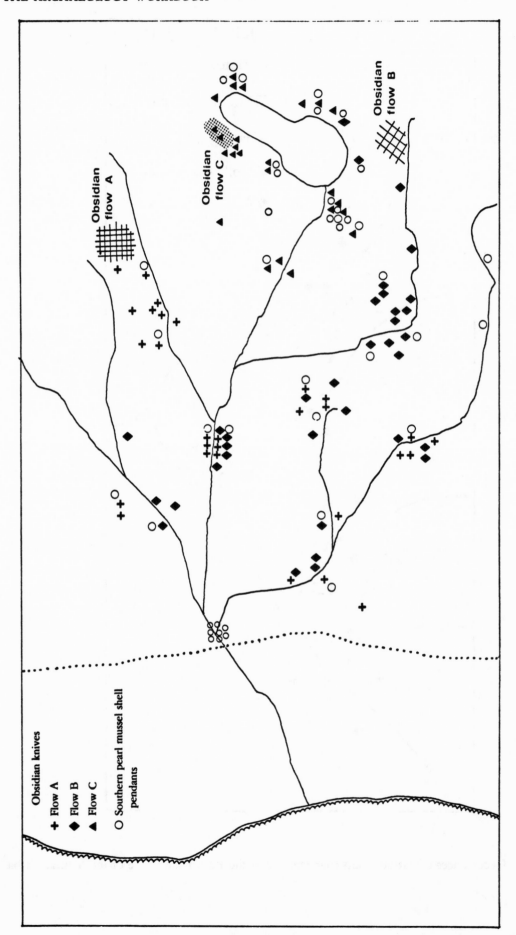

**Figure 6.3.    The distribution of obsidian knives and southern pearl mussel pendants in the Amontillado basin**

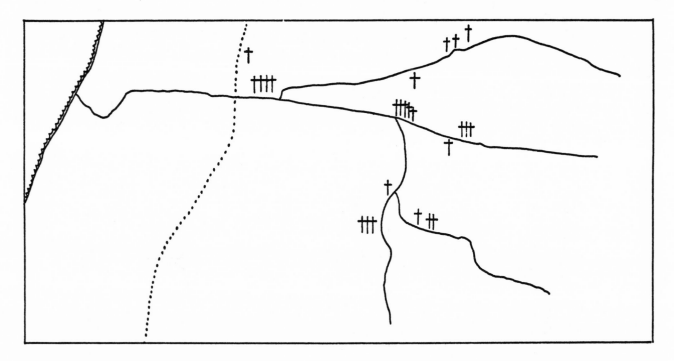

**Figure 6.4.** Distribution of imported northern-style bronze knives in the Oloroso basin

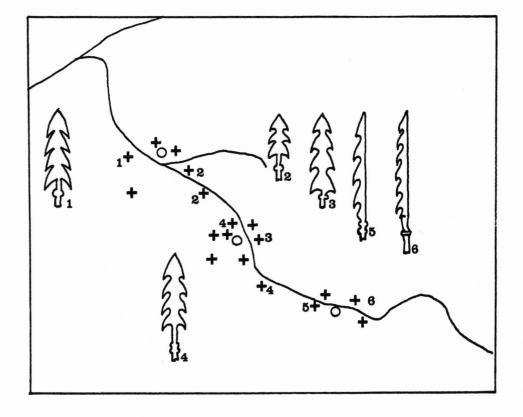

**Figure 6.5.** Dominant forms of bone harpoon at selected sites on the Rio Amontillado del Sur

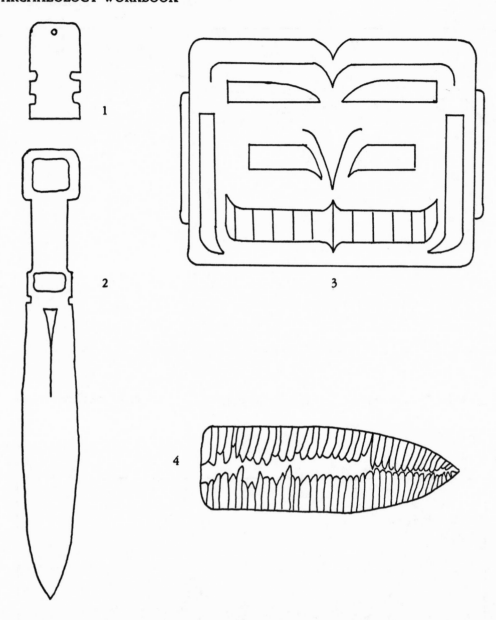

**Figure 6.6.**   Artifacts of the Sierra de la Serenidad Complex: (1) Southern pearl mussel shell pendant; (2) Northern style bronze knife; (3) Engraved jade plaque; (4) Obsidian knife

# The Adrar Abu

The Adrar Abu (figure 7.1) is a highland massif in the central Sahara Desert that rises to 3,643 meters above sea level. Because of its altitude, it receives a little winter rainfall on its northern slopes, and the summer monsoon brings some precipitation to the southern part of the massif. The rains permit the growth of a sparse steppic vegetation, with Mediterranean elements predominating in the north and sub-Saharan species in the south. Small herds of gazelle range over the massif, and there are a few desert-adapted carnivore and rodent species.

To the south of the Adrar, within the fossil shoreline of former Lake Carnot, is an oasis occupied by the TinHarar, a group who show a combination of Negroid and Caucasoid physical characteristics and who used to act as middlemen in the trans-Saharan caravan trade. They cultivate bulrush millet *(Pennisetum americanum)* and dates and work as laborers for the Bight Oil Company.

In the 1850s Barchan von Erg became the first European to visit the massif since Roman times. He suggested that a fragment from the *Geographia Mundi* of Felix Errator (*fl.* A.D. 125) may refer to the Adrar: "Mons Abitur is the land of carbuncles which are brought thence to the market of Sukkar by the Troglodytes, a race of Aethiopes. Before the destruction of Carthage these stones were cheap, but they are now beyond price and must be sought with much travail in the southlands."

During the colonial period, officers of the French Camel Corps mapped the region, noting the presence of numerous cairns, roughly built of stone and widely scattered over the Adrar. Lieutenant Farfouilleur dug out many of these and showed that they were burials, some of which contained Carthaginian or Roman artifacts (see fig. 7.1).

The WAWA (West African Women Archaeologists) expedition of 1985 made a survey in the area and carried out test excavations at Hassi Eni, an open site near the Lake Carnot shoreline, and Uan Tuh, a cave on the northern side of the massif. Their preliminary report is summarized below.

Hassi Eni has five archaeological layers. At its largest, which appears from surface indications to correspond to the period of Layers 2 and 3, it extended over three hectares. Four large test pits were excavated, in only one of which was the earliest occupation—Layer 5—represented. The final occupation,

**BACKGROUND INFORMATION:**

**ARCHAEO-LOGICAL DATA:**

**1. Hassi Eni**

55

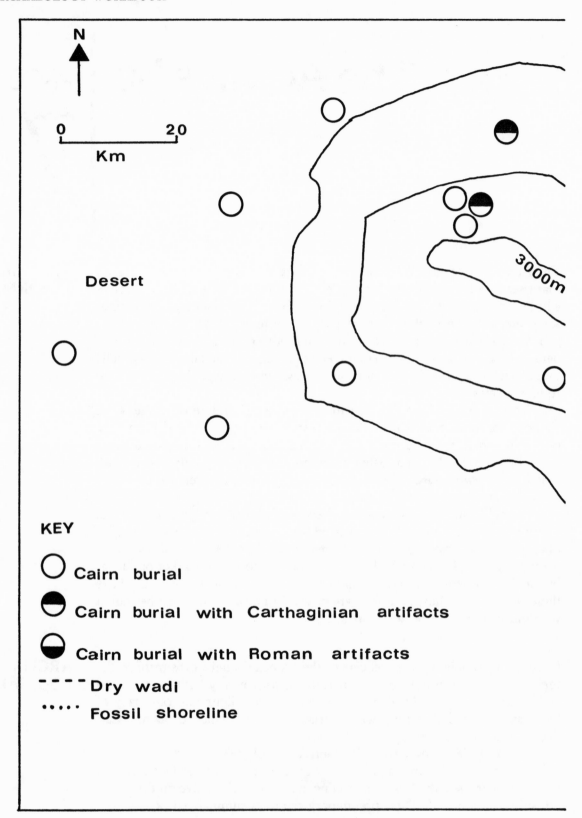

**Figure 7.1.** The Adrar Abu massif

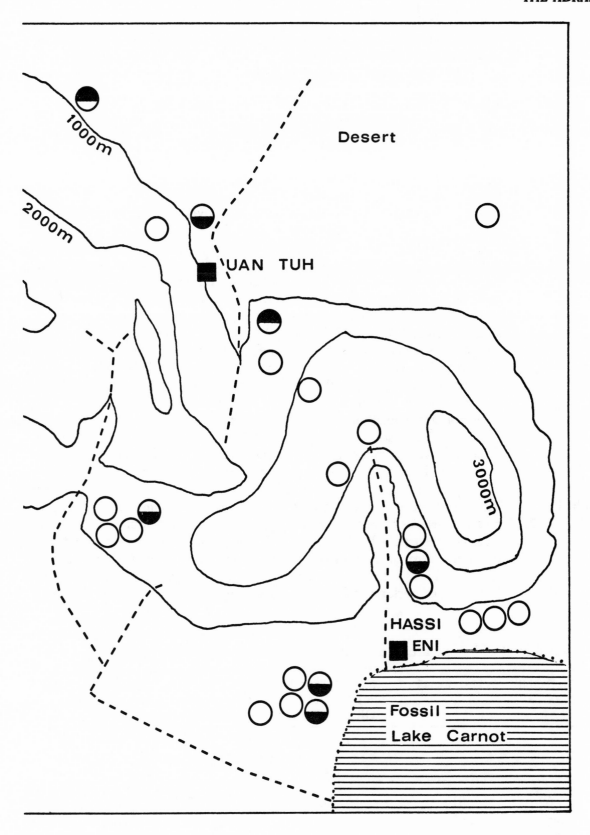

covering one hectare, is at the surface and takes the form of fifteen distinct artifact clusters enclosed within a dry stone wall three meters thick and standing up to two meters in height.

The deposits are described as follows:

| Layer | Thickness | Description |
|---|---|---|
| 1 | 10–15 cm. | Yellow eolian sand |
| 2 | 25 cm. | Yellowish-brown sandy loam |
| 3 | 30 cm. | Dark reddish-brown clayey loam, grading to black clay within the fossil shoreline |
| 4 | 15 cm. | Reddish-brown soil |
| 5 | 22 cm. | Reddened dune sand overlying unaltered sterile yellow dune sand |

Table 7.1 sets out the occurrence of flaked stone artifacts, pottery, and radiocarbon dates by layer. The flaked stone component, comprising quartz and chert raw materials, includes relatively few shaped tools, these being mainly microlithic lunates, triangles, and trapezes, together with an important scraper element. In Layer 2 there are 82 bifacially worked, tanged or hollow-based arrowheads. A large bored stone and fragments of ground stone axes were found in Layer 5, the latter type continuing into Layers 4, 3, and 2. Grindstones are present in the top three layers. Layer 3 is characterized also by the presence of bone harpoons and numerous small bored stones, Layer 1 by iron arrowheads and heavy metal picks.

Table 7.2 describes the faunal remains. Numerous small middens found in Layer 3 were composed largely of the bones of *Spinifex tepidus,* a fish that lives in shallow water and grows to no more than 9 centimeters in length.

**2. Uan Tuh (figure 7.2)**   The back wall of the cave at Uan Tuh, smoothed at some time in the past by sand particles driven by the wind, is decorated with paintings and engravings. There are polychrome paintings of herds of cattle and of men armed with bows and arrows. Paintings in black outline are highly stylized, showing sticklike figures riding camels and an airplane. The engravings, made by a technique of pecking and polishing, represent big game animals, including

**TABLE 7.1.** Hassi Eni: flaked stone artifacts, pottery, and radiocarbon dates by layer

| LAYER | FLAKED STONE ARTIFACTS | POTSHERDS | PERCENTAGE FREQUENCIES OF DECORATIVE TECHNIQUES OR MOTIFS ON POTSHERDS | | | | RADIOCARBON DATES |
|---|---|---|---|---|---|---|---|
| | | | WAVY LINE | DOTTED WAVY LINE | FIBER IMPRESSED | OTHER | |
| 1 | 6 | 813 | — | 30 | 48 | 22* | 200 ± 25 A.D. 260 ± 85 B.C. |
| 2 | 1289 | 4963 | 7 | 34 | 59 | — | |
| 3 | 1409 | 5818 | 22 | 73 | 3 | 2 | 6250 ± 200 B.C. |
| 4 | 24,374 | 269 | 79 | 10 | — | 11 | 7500 ± 800 B.C. |
| 5 | 6965 | 4 | 75 | 25 | — | — | 6400 ± 200 B.C. |

*includes rare specimens of *terra sigillata*

TABLE 7.2.   The fauna of Hassi Eni: minimum numbers of individuals by level (excepting fish and shellfish)

| | LEVEL | | | | |
| | 5 | 4 | 3 | 2 | 1 |
|---|---|---|---|---|---|
| Elephant | 4 | 2 | — | — | — |
| Rhinoceros | 1 | — | — | — | — |
| Hippopotamus | — | 8 | 32 | — | — |
| Giraffe | 2 | 6 | — | 1 | — |
| Bushbuck | 2 | 33 | 2 | — | — |
| Waterbuck | — | 13 | 29 | — | — |
| Gazelle | 1 | — | — | 18 | 55 |
| Unidentified large bovine | — | — | — | 89 | — |
| Unidentified bovids | 5 | 10 | — | 1 | — |
| Sheep/Goat | — | — | — | 14 | 146 |
| Warthog | 2 | — | 7 | 4 | — |
| Rock hyrax | 1 | 8 | 5 | 6 | 1 |
| Gerbil | — | — | — | 1 | 10 |
| Baboon | 1 | 3 | — | 4 | — |
| Lion | — | 3 | — | 3 | — |
| Hyena | 1 | 9 | 4 | 12 | 2 |
| Jackal | 2 | — | — | 8 | 1 |
| Crocodile | — | — | 16 | — | — |
| Ostrich | 1 | 3 | — | 8 | 4 |
| Catfish | — | — | many | 4 | — |
| *Spinifex tepidus* | — | — | v.many | — | — |
| Freshwater mussels | — | 6 | v.many | 16 | 3 |

elephants and buffalo *(Bubalus antiquus);* there is one jackal-headed anthropomorphic figure. It was noted that in one case the painting of a man's head obscured part of an engraving. A slab fallen from the cave wall showing traces of red and yellow paint was found in Layer 2, and the hoofs of one of the cows are covered by Layer 1 deposits.

A test trench was dug perpendicular to the back wall, extending forward through part of the talus on the platform below the cave.

Inside the cave, Layer 3 contained a poor quartz component that included microlithic lunates and triangles. A smaller number of other tools shows signs of polishing by wind action and differing typological characteristics; among the latter, tanged and triangular points are represented together with sidescrapers and tanged endscrapers. Only wavy line and dotted wavy line motifs are found on the sherds from this layer. No bone was preserved either in Layer 3 or in Layer 2.

There is a marked decrease in the density of finds within Layer 2 from its base to the almost sterile upper part. A charcoal sample consisting of carbonized seeds (18 spp. of wild grasses have been provisionally identified), found in a large pot decorated with fiber impressions, gave a date of 3600 ± 150 B.C. Various forms of bifacially worked and hollow-based arrowheads are present in the flaked stone component, while the potsherds show 78% fiber impressions, 8% dotted wavy line, and 14% comb-impressed punctations. Grinding equipment is common, and there are 6 ground stone axes.

Flaked stone is not present in Layer 1. There are, on the other hand, numerous fragments of iron tools, including picks, hammers, and wedges.

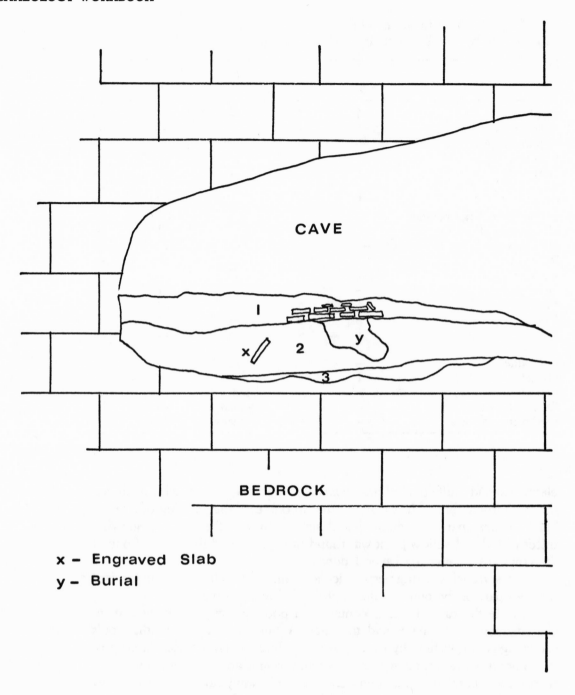

x - Engraved Slab
y - Burial

Figure 7.2.    Uan Tuh: section

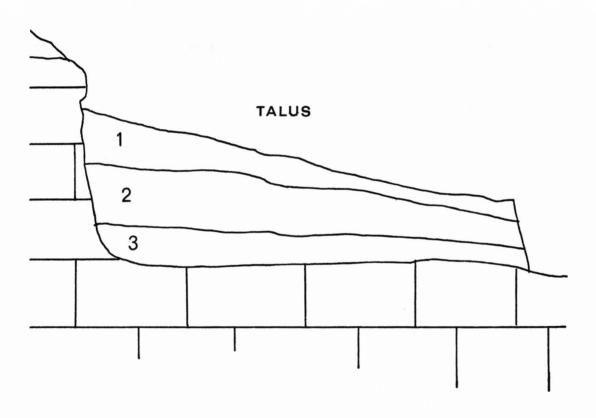

The pottery is mainly decorated with fiber impressions. From this layer came a Carthaginian coin struck in 147 B.C. At the base of the level was found the burial of a woman wearing a necklace of iron beads; a single red gem stone was found some 20 centimeters above the pubic symphysis. Sheep and/or goat bones are common; gazelle is the only other animal represented.

The only available information on the sequence from the talus is as follows:

Layer 1   Flaked quartz artifacts, iron tools, and pottery present

Layer 2   Sterile (eolian sand)

Layer 3   Stone component includes no microliths or bifacially worked arrowheads, but there is a large flake element made by prepared core techniques. Tanged tools are present. Radiocarbon date of 22,500 ± 400 B.C. Bones of hippopotamus, reedbuck, and waterbuck

Attempt a concise reconstruction of the prehistory of the Adrar Abu massif. Pay special attention to definition of the environmental sequence and its relationship, if any, to the cultural phases represented. What can be said about prehistoric economy in this region?

# The Pitts River Basin and the Wulliweela Range

## PROBLEM 8

**BACKGROUND INFORMATION:**

The Pitts River basin lies in northwestern Australia, and the Pitts flows into the Timor Sea (figure 8.1). The vegetation in the basin is subtropical grassland with scattered scrub and eucalypts. To the north, the basin is bounded by the sharply rising Wulliweela (Lame Fox) range, with peaks topping 3,000 feet; to the south, the land rises more gently but becomes increasingly arid until, about 50 miles south of the river, the grassland is seasonal or intermittent, reverting to desert in periods of low rainfall. Along the coast,

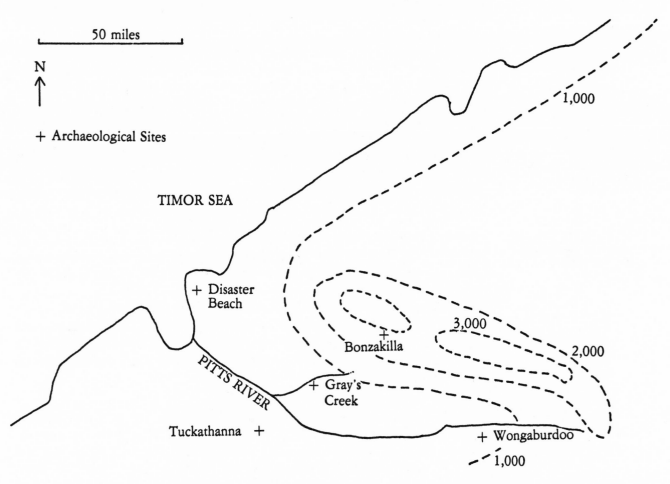

**Figure 8.1.** The Pitts valley and the Wulliweela range

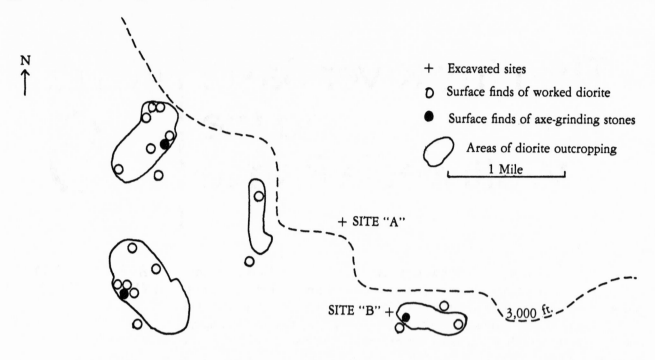

N

+  Excavated sites

◻  Surface finds of worked diorite

●  Surface finds of axe-grinding stones

⬭  Areas of diorite outcropping

1 Mile

+ SITE "A"

SITE "B" +

3,000 ft.

Figure 8.2.   The Bonzakilla complex

from the mouth of the Pitts and stretching northwards, are mangrove swamps.

Today the region is economically dependent on large-scale sheep farming in the Pitts valley and on a large iron ore plant on the northern side of the Wulliweelas. Due to intensive competition from sheep, large wild animals are now scarce in the Pitts basin, but early European farmers' reports describe the area as being exceptionally rich in kangaroo and other fauna. Shellfish are plentiful along the swampy coasts, and dugong, a large sea mammal, has been sighted off the mouth of the Pitts.

**ARCHAEO-LOGICAL DATA:** The archaeological evidence presented here is a summary of the results of ten years' work by the Pitts River Archaeological Society, a small but enthusiastic group led by their chairman, Sheila Karminsky, a local schoolteacher.

Figure 8.1 shows the archaeological sites at which excavations have been carried out. Three of these, Gray's Creek, Tuckathanna, and Wongaburdoo, may be described as valley sites, while Disaster Beach is coastal. High up in the Wulliweela range is the Bonzakilla complex, at which two excavations were carried out.

**Bonzakilla** The Bonzakilla complex lies around the 3,000 foot mark in the western Wulliweelas. Two sites, "A" and "B," have been excavated, and members of the society have walked intensively over the area shown in figure 8.2 and collected surface materials. The great majority of the latter consists of waste flakes of diorite, along with a smaller number of axe-shaped roughouts and complete edge-ground stone axes, also of diorite. Locations where one or more such pieces have been found are marked on figure 8.2, which also shows areas where diorite outcrops have been located. A further feature shown is the occurrence of a number of small boulders, about two feet high, the tops of which are artificially smoothed and slightly concave.

## BONZAKILLA "A":

This is a shallow rock shelter, the rear wall of which is decorated with a painted figure in red (figure 8.3), the only known example of rock art in the Wulliweelas. A 3 × 2 yard trench dug into the deposit immediately beneath this figure reached a depth of 19 inches before hitting bedrock and produced a few stone tools, among which were an edge-ground axe and some geometric microliths. Also of interest was a pendant of oyster shell, of a species common along the Timor Sea coast.

## BONZAKILLA "B":

This excavation was dug into the filling of a narrow cleft just below a concave, smoothed boulder. A sketch of the north face of this trench appears in figure 8.4. Three distinct artifactual layers were found separated by sterile deposit. In Layer 1 (the top layer) and in Layer 3 were found concentrations of charcoal extending into the north face as shown. Samples from these gave dates of 2900 ± 100 B.P. for Layer 1 and 2650 ± 120 B.P. for Layer 3. All

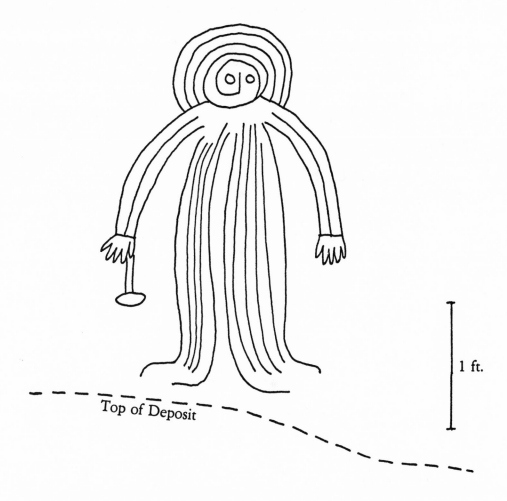

1 ft.

**Figure 8.3.** Schematic drawing on the rear wall of the Bonzakilla "A" rockshelter

three layers contained numerous stone artifacts, predominant among which were axe roughouts and flaking debris of diorite.

**Disaster Beach**  The Disaster Beach site consists of a low but extensive midden 5.2 yards above and set back some 200 yards inland from the current high tide line. The midden, only some 3 feet thick, is almost entirely composed of broken and compacted shells of *Cardium sp.* with smaller amounts of other edible shellfish shells. A grid of 2 × 2 yard squares was laid out and alternate squares dug to a total of twenty. There was no detectable stratigraphy, and the sections have not been reproduced. Three radiocarbon dates were run on shell samples taken from three different squares. These gave:

| | |
|---|---|
| SID–0021 | Modern |
| SID–5467 | 4000 ± 250 B.P. |
| SID–5468 | 4600 ± 400 B.P. |

The numerous stone artifacts from the site included edge-ground stone axes, scrapers, and unifacial points. Thirty-two double-ended bone points were also found and three kangaroo femurs, all of which had been split longitudinally.

**Gray's Creek**  The site on Gray's Creek was discovered when flash flooding eroded the creek bank to reveal a horizontal line of bone and stone objects. A second freak rainstorm destroyed the site completely about a month later, but a salvage excavation mounted by the P.R.A.S. had by then demonstrated the existence of a buried land surface on which were lying a number of stone tools, the majority being unifacial points and scrapers, and bones that must have come from at least seven adult grey kangaroos *(Macropus giganteus)*. Particularly striking was one skull with a geometric microlith embedded in

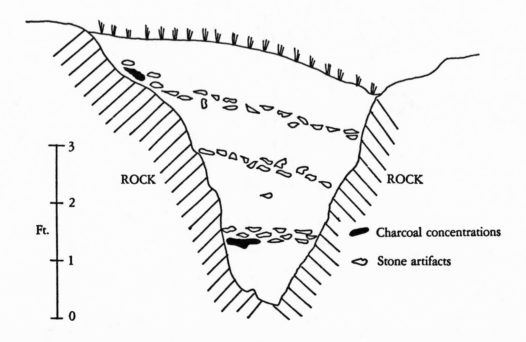

ROCK                    ROCK

Ft.

⬛ Charcoal concentrations

▱ Stone artifacts

**Figure 8.4.**  Sketch map of the north face of the trial trench at Bonzakilla "B"

the occiput, the wound evidently not having been immediately fatal, since there was new bone growth around the microlith. One exotic find was a pendant of baler shell (figure 8.5), the natural range of this species being limited to the shores of the Cape York peninsula, over 1,000 miles to the east.

Similar in some ways to Gray's Creek, the **Wongaburdoo** site was discovered while digging foundations for new sheep-shearing sheds. Artifacts are scattered at a depth of 4 feet 3 inches to 4 feet 8 inches over an area of about 12 × 15 yards. Large numbers of kangaroo bones were found (see table

**Wongaburdoo**

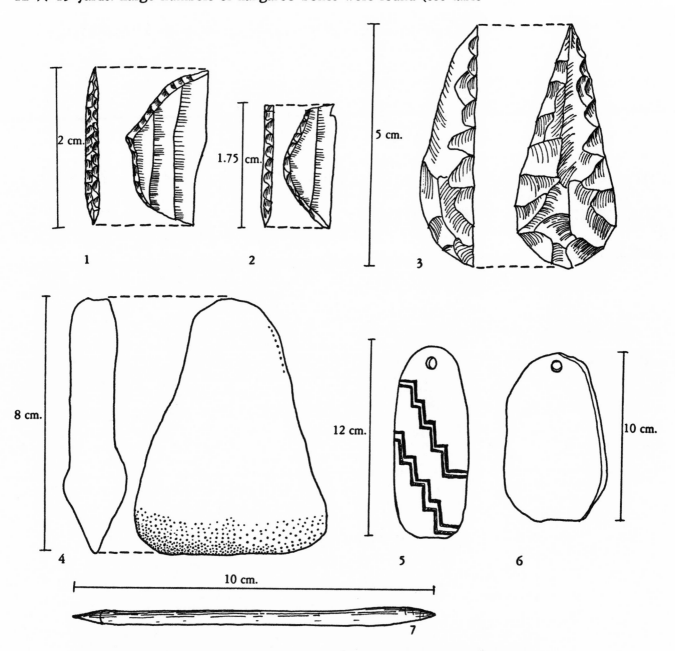

**Figure 8.5. Artifacts from the Pitts River area** 1. Geometric microlith (Tuckathanna) 2.Geometric microlith (Bonzakilla "B," Layer 2) 3. Unifacial point (Bonzakilla "B," Layer 3) 4. Edge-ground stone axe (Disaster Beach) 5. Pendant of oyster shell (Bonzakilla "A") 6. Pendant of baler shell (Gray's Creek) 7. Bone point (Disaster Beach)

8.2), and it was noted that the skulls had suffered *post mortem* splitting and crushing. There were also a number of geometric microliths, scrapers, and an edge-ground diorite axe. Despite careful excavation, no post molds or other signs of structures could be identified.

**Tuckathanna**   Tuckathanna was discovered when Mrs. Karminsky's dog scraped up a microlith while going after a rabbit. A 2 × 4 yard test trench revealed a single layer of artifactual material but gave no indication of its horizontal extent. The stone artifacts include 38 microliths and 2 diorite flakes. No bones were found except for 1 kangaroo humerus; a charcoal sample gave a date of 4500 ± 500 B.P. (SID–6289).

A quantitative analysis of stone artifacts from all the excavated sites is contained in table 8.1, while figure 8.5 shows typical specimens of tool types. Table 8.2 shows the anatomical composition of the *Macropus* remains from Wongaburdoo and Gray's Creek.

**TABLE 8.1.   Stone artifacts recovered from sites in the Pitts River basin and the Wulliweela range**

| ARTIFACT TYPES & RAW MATERIALS | BONZAKILLA "A" | BONZAKILLA "B" 1 | 2 | 3 | DISASTER BEACH | GRAY'S CREEK | WONGABURDOO | TUCKATHANNA |
|---|---|---|---|---|---|---|---|---|
| *Chert & Quartz* | | | | | | | | |
| Scrapers | — | 1 | — | — | 12 | 9 | 16 | 3 |
| Geometric microliths | 5 | — | 3 | — | — | 1 | 28 | 38 |
| Unifacial points | — | 4 | 1 | 6 | 2 | 16 | — | — |
| Cores | 2 | 8 | 6 | 14 | 124 | 3 | 6 | 14 |
| Waste flakes | 12 | 68 | 55 | 92 | 6,042 | 27 | 14 | 262 |
| *Diorite* | | | | | | | | |
| Edge-ground axes | 1 | 3 | 6 | 1 | 3 | — | 1 | — |
| Roughouts | — | 17 | 10 | 23 | 4 | — | — | — |
| Waste flakes | 2 | 216 | 449 | 317 | 63 | — | — | 2 |

**TABLE 8.2.   Bones of *Macropus giganteus* from Gray's Creek and Wongaburdoo**

| BODY PARTS | GRAY'S CREEK | WONGABURDOO |
|---|---|---|
| Ribs | 60 | 104 |
| Cervical, Thoracic, and Lumbar Vertebrae | 69 | 62 |
| Skulls | 7 | 10 |
| Metatarsals | — | 20 |
| Ulna-radii | — | 14 |
| Other miscellaneous small bones | 32 | 40 |

You should by now be learning to recognize the significant questions inherent in a body of archaeological data. How do you then account for the variability in the archaeological record described above?

# PROBLEM 9 | Uhuru

Uhuru is an administrative division of the country of Duduwa. It lies on one of the African Rift valleys (figure 9.1a). From the Salt Lake shores, thick thorn scrub reaches back to the rift escarpment, pierced only by the narrow valley of the Diyam River. Above the escarpment stretch the savannas of the Labi Plateau, gently rolling country with a mosaic of edaphic (natural) grassland and thorn thickets. Both the well-watered plateau and the dry bush below the scarp are infested with tsetse fly (*Glossina* spp.), carriers of trypanosomes that cause sleeping sickness in man and *nagana* in cattle. These diseases are usually fatal.

The Labi Plateau is densely populated by the Gora, Bantu-speaking farmers organized into powerful chiefdoms. An epic recited by the court historian on the most solemn ritual occasions relates that the present Paramount is the thirty-second in line from the founding ancestor, Urmuntu, who, with his two brothers and their wives, canoed along a great river through deep forest, finally debouching onto open plains. (Whether this story is to be taken literally or not is hotly disputed by folklorists, some of whom claim to have detected a Freudian and others a duplex structuralist content.) After living there for twenty-three generations and multiplying "like hares" *(Lepus capensis),* internecine warfare caused Angora, ancestor of the present Paramount, to lead a section of the tribe eastward to the territory they occupy today, which, it is claimed, they found uninhabited. Subsidiary versions of the epic told in some lesser chiefdoms agree on the earlier and perhaps mythological epoch but differ on later episodes and in particular the genealogy of the Paramount.

The land beneath the escarpment is sparsely occupied by Gora migrants and a few Hero, known to the Gora as *wa-goba-sitopa,* or 'those who mutilate their mouths'. The Hero speak a Southern Sudanic language unrelated to Bantu and live as hunters and from the products of their sheep and goats. They are noted for their unique combination of cycling age sets and semi-segmentary lineages that S. Below, author of the definitive monograph on Gora fertility and rainmaking cults, argues are relics of a period when their population was much larger than today.

The earliest historical record dates from 1724 when the Reverend Ludd, who died three years later of a "wasting consumptive lethargy," first crossed the Salt Lake:

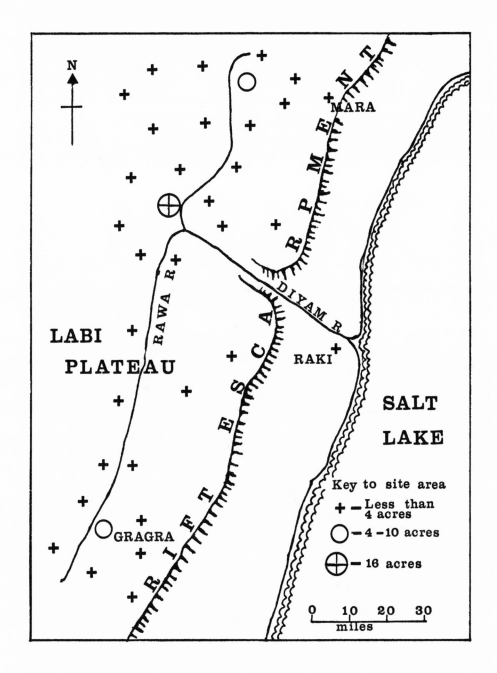

**Figure 9.1a.** The Uhuru division of the Republic of Duduwa showing the distribution of sites with graphite burnished wares

Nearing the strand we espied the smoke of many fires and alighting at the mouth of a river, called by my amanuensis the Jam, marched upstream along a narrow bosky way. Suddenly we came upon a camp of which the denizens were women and children only who, seeing my pale countenance, fled with lamentations into the enclosing forest. Upon entering one of their straw hovels I found an ancient dissembling himself beneath a pile of stinking goatskins whom, being questioned, told us that his tribe, the Hayrose, lived in great fear of the Garboes of the western mountains. For many years the warriors of his tribe had led Arabs into the hills to raid for slaves. For this

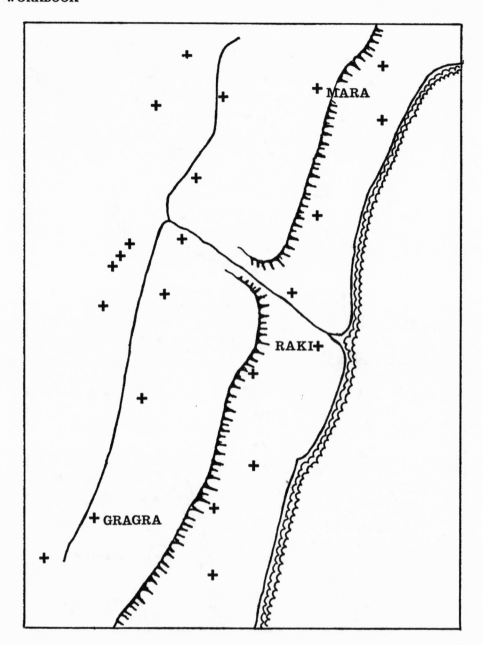

**Figure 9.1b.**   Distribution of sites with mat-impressed pottery

treachery the Hayrose received from the Arabs silver but from the Garboes enmity and death. Of late the King upon the mountain had entered into league with an Arab to enslave his own people. May the Good Lord forgive them!

**ARCHAEO-
LOGICAL DATA:** In 1922 a settler turned up some interesting finds at Mara on the plateau. He had a gang of laborers dig there for a week and, in *Uhuru Notes and Records,* reported finding a smelting furnace, the skeleton of a cow, and pottery, some with a shining black finish, some "with a pattern of raised dots and other designs in a lightly depressed band," and other pieces that appeared to have

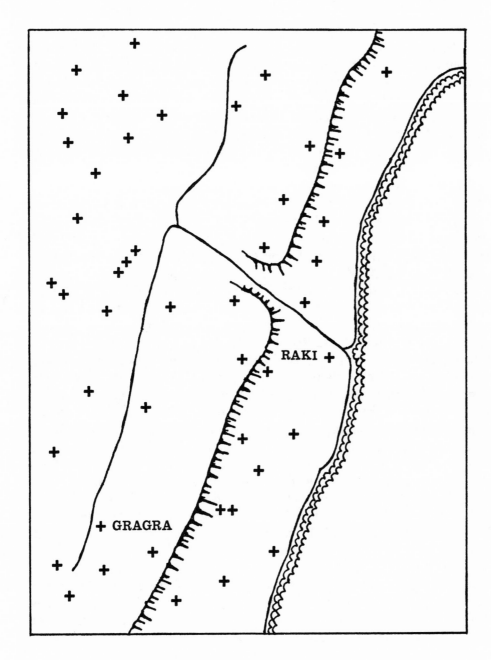

**Figure 9.1c.** Distribution of sites giving stone bowls

been "rolled on a native carpet before firing." He also mentioned the presence of small cylinders of marble, which he termed gaming pieces but which comparative ethnographic evidence suggests are, in fact, ornaments worn in the ear, nose, or lip.

In 1960 the Duduwa Antiquities Service instituted an intensive survey of the district, later publishing three maps (figures 9.1a–c) showing the distribution of graphite-burnished pottery, mat-impressed wares, and stone bowls. Surface areas of sites are also grossly indicated. Two sites were subsequently selected for excavation, and the results of these digs are summarized in the following notes, tables, and figures.

**1. Gragra**     Gragra, a cluster of low mounds of sizes varying between 23 × 44 feet and 47 × 88 feet and elliptical in shape, is located in the valley of the Rawa in the southern part of the plateau. A large test trench (10 × 38 feet) was excavated in one of the larger mounds and, because no natural stratigraphy could be recognized, was dug in arbitrary horizontal levels or spits, each one-foot deep. After the section (figure 9.2) had dried out, various features could be identified, including the stumps of mud walls, beaten earth floors, and silos. It was also noted that an old land surface formed by a minor erosional episode passed diagonally across spits 3 and 4.

Table 9.1 sets out the distribution of various decorative techniques on pottery from the excavation and of C[14] dates by spit. Spits 6 and 7 contained stone bowl fragments, grindstones, polished stone axes, and other flaked stone tools. In spit 7, animal bones included 33% sheep and/or goats, 15% cattle, and 52% wild animals. In spit 6 the frequencies were, respectively: 12%, 69%, and 12%. Marble and bone iip plugs are present in small numbers in spits 6 and 5, and there is a fragmentary specimen in spit 4. Besides the appearance of pottery in spit 5, carbonized seeds of a cultivated race of guineacorn *(Sorghum bicolor)* were recovered. Unfortunately, the bones from spit 5 were lost when a Land Rover overturned and burned while en route to base. Spit 4 contains both flaked and polished stone tools and grinding equipment, but stone bowls are no longer present. Two iron fragments were found in the northeastern corner of the trench. Eighty-six percent of the bones are of wild species, the remainder of cattle and ovicaprids. Remains of domestic architecture and underground silos are found in spits 3 and above. Grindstones are also present in these levels but, except in parts of spit 3, other stone tools are entirely absent. The fauna is composed of wild animals, save for a few goat remains. Iron tools become more common in these levels, and in spit 2 there is iron slag. Spits 1 and 2 also produced fragments of ivory, intricately worked in geometric designs and motifs derived from Arabic calligraphy. Coins with inscriptions in Arabic found in a hoard buried in a roulette decorated pot were all minted between A.D. 1610 and 1783.

**2. Raki rock shelter**     Raki rock shelter, located on the lower course of the Diyam River, was excavated by natural layers under the direction of Ms. A. Dambo, a new recruit to the Antiquities Service, using secondary school pupils as her labor force. She describes the stratigraphy (figure 9.3) as follows:

**TABLE 9.1.**   **Gragra: percentages of decorative techniques on pottery and radiocarbon dates by spit**

| SPIT | | PERCENTAGES OF DECORATIVE TECHNIQUES ON POTTERY | | | | | C[14] DATES |
|------|-------------|---------------|---------|-----------|----------------------|-------------------|----------------|
| | NO. SHERDS | MAT-IMPRESSED | INCISED | ROULETTED | GRAPHITE BURNISHED | PLAIN & UNIDENT. | |
| 1 | 6590 | 2 | 2 | 43 | 40 | 13 | |
| 2 | 8828 | 1 | 3 | 50 | 37 | 19 | A.D. 1600 ± 40 |
| 3 | 6651 | 8 | 8 | 48 | 29 | 7 | |
| 4 | 2797 | 51 | 22 | 12 | 3 | 12 | A.D. 830 ± 75 |
| 5 | 1462 | 40 | 24 | — | — | 36 | A.D. 370 ± 50 |
| 6 | — | — | — | — | — | — | |
| 7 | — | — | — | — | — | — | 830 ± 75 B.C. |

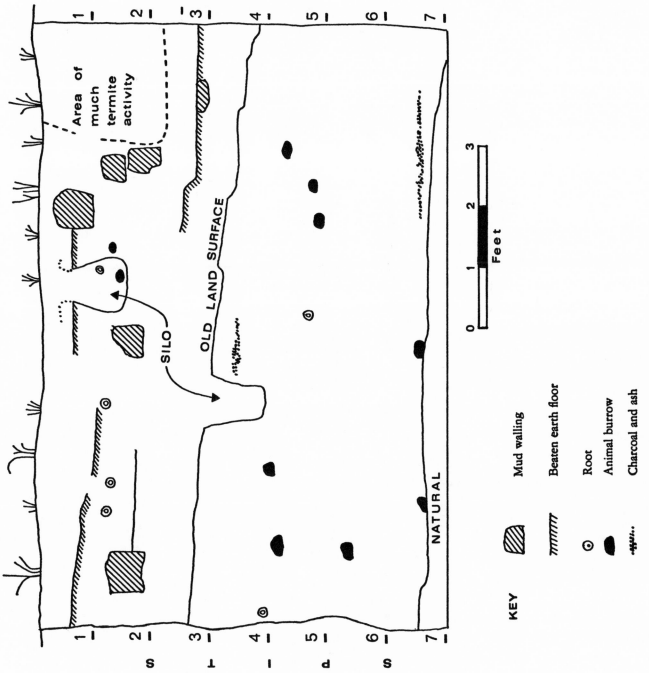

Figure 9.2. Gragra: north wall section

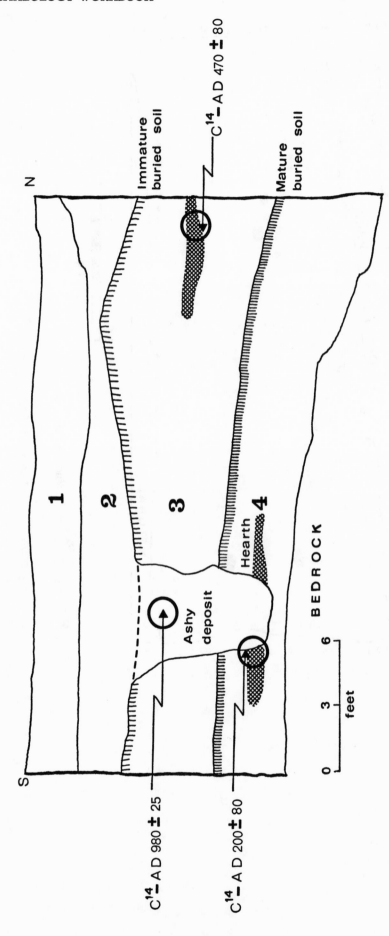

Figure 9.3. Raki rock shelter section

TABLE 9.2. The fauna of Raki rock shelter: minimum numbers of individuals by layer and species

| SPECIES | LAYER | | | |
|---|---|---|---|---|
| | 4 | 3 | 2 | 1 |
| Elephant | 2 | — | 1 | — |
| Rhinoceros | 1 | 1 | — | — |
| Roan antelope | 5 | 1 | 1 | — |
| Grant's gazelle | 3 | 1 | 3 | 4 |
| Thompson's gazelle | 6 | 2 | — | — |
| Impala | 2 | 2 | 2 | 1 |
| Eland | 1 | 3 | — | 2 |
| Wildebeest | 4 | 1 | 2 | 1 |
| Duiker | — | — | 2 | 5 |
| Cattle | — | 8 | — | — |
| Ovicaprids | — | 18 | 14 | 10 |
| Zebra | 1 | 2 | — | 2 |
| Leopard | — | 1 | — | — |
| Honey badger | 1 | — | — | — |
| Dog | — | 2 | 1 | 3 |
| Totals | 26 | 42 | 26 | 28 |

Layer 1. Grey dusty deposit with a few angular granite inclusions of various sizes

Layer 2. Light reddish-brown gritty deposit, inclusions touching, small and subangular to angular. At the base of the layer a pit with ashy fill, difficult to distinguish at base from the Layer 4 hearth

Layer 3. Top foot is dark reddish-brown (immature buried soil), grading to reddish-brown below. Inclusions are rare, small and subrounded to rounded. Some charcoal streaks

Layer 4. Top 18 inches is very dark grey-brown (mature buried soil), grading to dark grey-brown loam; inclusions very rare, rounded or disintegrating *in situ*. Numerous carbonaceous lenticules and one definite hearth

Layer 4 produced a poor assemblage (1,302 pieces, 96 tools) of flaked stone and a polished stone axe fragment from near the top of the level. The fauna includes elephant, zebra, and various antelopes. A human skeleton from the layer has been studied by eminent physical anthropologists from London and Nairobi, who describe it as showing an "advanced Neanderthaloid and proto-Negroid" combination of features. Layer 3 contains flaked and polished stone, a stone bowl fragment, and a few sherds of incised pottery. Layer 2 produced two stone bowls, both mat-impressed and incised pottery, and a few heavily corroded iron fragments. Layer 1 has given a similar assemblage differing only in the absence of stone tools and in the presence of two sherds of glazed pottery decorated with Arabic inscriptions of the sixteenth-seventeenth centuries. Details of the fauna are set out in table 9.2, and radiocarbon determinations and the locations from which the samples were taken are indicated on the section (figure 9.3).

After a careful study of the evidence, and having paid special attention to data quality, write a concise outline account of the archaeology of Uhuru. Special consideration should be given to changes in prehistoric economy and their causation.

# The Lon Gon Bronzes

The great East Asian state of Kwangchung has one of the oldest homogeneous cultural traditions in the world and has long been considered the seminal area for urban and literate culture in the eastern parts of Asia (figure 10.1). Recorded Kwangchung history goes back to about 1500 B.C., corresponding to the start of the Bronze Age in the area. This is preceded by a Neolithic of unknown duration, the staple crops being millet in north Kwangchung and rice in the south.

South of Kwangchung and bordered by the Pacific Ocean lies the region of Ankang, usually regarded by scholars as an area in which food production, metallurgy, and urban concentration were alike late and influenced by diffusion from southern Kwangchung. Until very recently, no hard evidence was available concerning the Neolithic of Ankang, and the earliest bronze artifacts were thought to be two vessels recovered without stratigraphical provenience from the port of Lon Gon and the inland city of Bao Lo. These vessels (figure 10.2: 1 and 2) are stylistically similar and have been termed the Lon Gon bronzes.

In 1984 and 1985, two excavations were carried out that may entail a complete revision of ideas on the relative priority of cultural developments in Kwangchung and Ankang. The problems raised are fascinating but tantalizing, since further work, or even reexamination of sections and finds, has been prevented by political developments in the area.

The following presentation gives a very brief outline of the historical information about Kwangchung and Ankang, summarizes the evidence from the excavations at Tai Pin and Rong Numba, and quotes excerpts from the views of two eminent authorities on the history of the area.

**HISTORICAL OUTLINE:**

Traditional Kwangchung history divides the Bronze Age into two political periods, the Pung Dynasty (c. 1500–1187 B.C.), during which the central power of the Pungs was extended to the limits of Kwangchung, and the Kong Dynasty (1187–526 B.C.), a period of peaceful consolidation and the growth of subsidiary power centers within Kwangchung. The dynasty came to an end when open warfare broke out between two of the secondary polities. The central authority proved ineffective in reestablishing its dominant position, and the five regional centers that vied for control have given their name to the Years of the Five Flowers (526–304 B.C.). During this time of continued unrest and frustrated imperial ambitions, the border states, including south

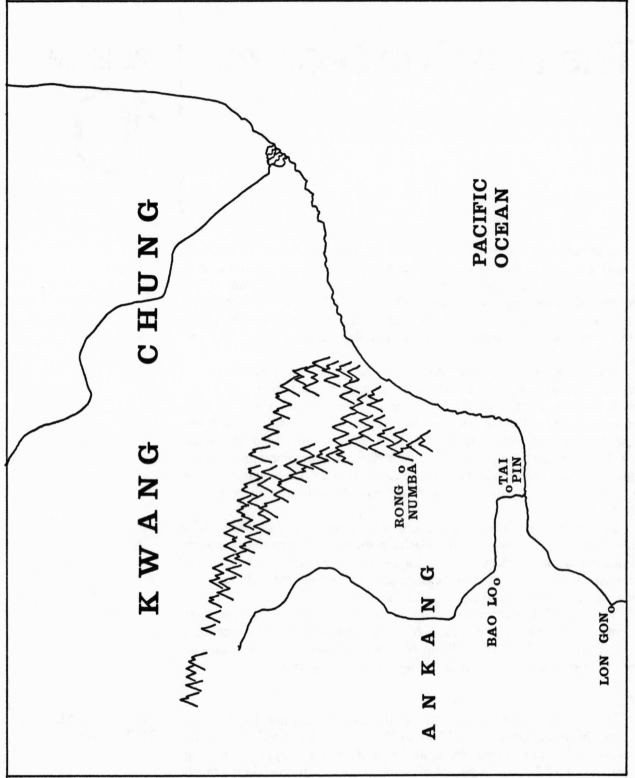

Figure 10.1.    Archaeological sites in Ankang

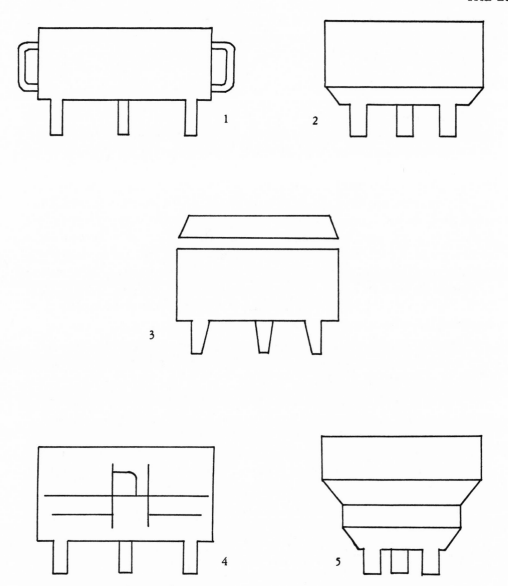

**Figure 10.2.** Vertical schematic views of the Lon Gon bronzes. All are circular in horizontal cross section and have tripod feet. 1. Bao Lo; 2. Lon Gon; 3. Rong Numba; 4. & 5. Tai Pin

Kwangchung, showed an increasing interest in extending their spheres of influence beyond the limits of Kwangchung proper. It was during this period that iron implements and weapons first came to be used in the area.

Among the most characteristic artifacts of Kwangchung during the last one-and-a-half millennia B.C. were bronze food vessels. These maintain a clear continuity of function and overall style but exhibit minor stylistic variation that can be correlated with the political periodization. Thus in the early historical archaeology of Kwangchung, the details of stylistic change have repeatedly been used, and with success, as chronological markers.

We are fortunate in having historical information concerning northern Ankang from the second century A.D. onwards. It is at this time that Hindu immigrants from India founded a state there, the name of which has been forgotten but whose first ruler is recorded as Dharmagupta. The extent of his territorial suzerainty is unknown. There are strong traditions, however, that his capital was located near the site of the modern city of Tai Pin at the mouth of the river Sing Hai.

## EXCAVATIONS IN 1984 AND 1985:

### Tai Pin

The Tai Pin excavation was intended to identify the city of Dharmagupta. After a complete survey of the historical and traditional sources concerning its location, the exact siting of the dig was decided on the strength of a bronze figure of the Hindu deity Siva, found by chance during the digging of an irrigation channel in the rice paddies. While it appears almost certain that the excavation was successful in determining the original site of the city, the underlying strata are those that have most aroused the interest of the academic community. Since the main trench was cut back from the side of an erosional feature, only one section is available (figure 10.3). The following is a commentary taken from the excavators' preliminary report, and it should be noted that where two stratigraphical units have the same letter but are differentiated by primes (e.g., A, A', A″), the excavators regarded the units as belonging to the same stratum but discontinuous in section because of accidents of deposition, features, and the like:

*Layer A:* Fine greyish to dark-grey silt. Finds were sparse but included pieces of concrete, fragments of iron sheet, and a French ten-sous piece dated 1907.

*Layers B & B':* Greyish-buff sand with silty lenses. Two wall stubs made of faced stone blocks project upwards into this level, and on the inner side of each is a rammed earth floor. Near the inner side of the wall in B was a portion of an engraved tablet with a fragmentary inscription (figure 10.6a). A charcoal sample from B' gave a date of A.D. 220 ± 50 (AoK-9326).

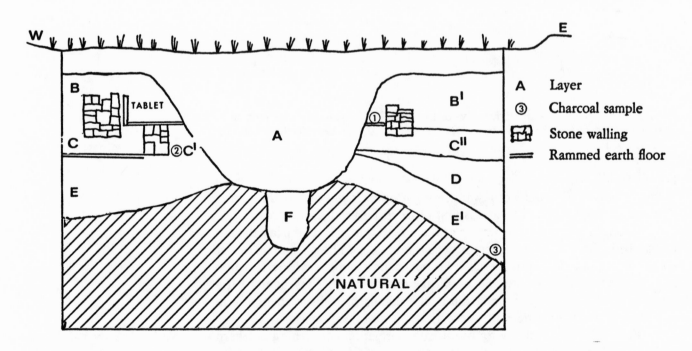

Figure 10.3.   Section of the excavation at Tai Pin

*Layers C, C', & C":* Dark brown with ashy inclusions. In C and C' there are also numerous lumps of rubble, both stone and fired mud. Many sherds of a thin-walled, well-fired black ware, decorated with stylized animal figures in a buff slip. The radiocarbon dating for a charcoal sample (location 2 on fig. 10.3) is 450 $\pm$ 125 B.C. (AoK-9327). The footings of the walls in B and B' project down into this layer, and another wall of faced stone blocks divides C from C'. The base of C is formed by a rammed earth floor.

*Layer D:* Light greyish-brown, very ashy and soft. Fragments of bone (water buffalo and pig identified). Sherds of a red ware with burnished surface, undecorated except around the rims where there are incised bands and occasional appliqué pellets.

*Layers E & E':* Compact reddish-brown deposit. A few sherds of a thick-walled ware with a very sandy paste and yellow in color. Most sherds are heavily eroded, but cord-impressed decoration is decipherable on a few pieces. Two ground stone axes. Charcoal from location 3 gave a date of 1800 $\pm$ 150 B.C. (AoK-9328).

*Layer F:* Pitfill, mottled black and dark brown, soft and moist. Pit contained two bronze vessels (one decorated) very similar in style to those from Lon Gon and Bao Lo (figure 10.2:4 & 5). The only other artifacts were two sherds of yellow sandy ware and a spall from a ground stone adze.

Rong Numba is a shallow rock shelter situated in the fertile valley of the headwaters of one of the lesser tributaries of the Sing Hai Ho system. A 2 × 2 meter sondage was dug into the surprisingly deep deposits a year after the Tai Pin excavation (figure 10.4). The nature of the deposit, a light ashy cave earth, was consistent throughout; the layers were distinguished only on the basis of slight color differences, visible during excavation. Their reality was retrospectively confirmed by reference to the contained artifacts. Radiocarbon samples were run by two highly respected laboratories, Neubergen (NBg) and Amo-Kron Isotopes Ltd (AoK), but gave two worryingly diverse series of dates (table 10.1). The excavator has given a brief statement of the artifactual content of the layers:

**Rong Numba**

*Layer A:* Fragments of grey pottery decorated with horizontal fluting.

*Layer B:* Well-fired black ware with buff slip resembling that from Tai Pin:C. A bronze vessel, lidded, and in the position shown on the section (figure 10.2:3).

*Layers C & C':* Red burnished ware similar to that from Tai Pin:D.

*Layer D:* Pit fill containing both black and red ware sherds.

*Layer E:* Yellow sandy ware with cord impressions, also several pieces of slag from copper smelting. Several sherds show impressions of cultivated rice grains.

*Layer F:* Yellow sandy ware, but sparser than in E. Three pieces of "D"-sectioned ground stone axes. One nearly complete pot contained a mass of carbonized seeds, among which have been identified those of two wild trees bearing edible fruit, and seeds of

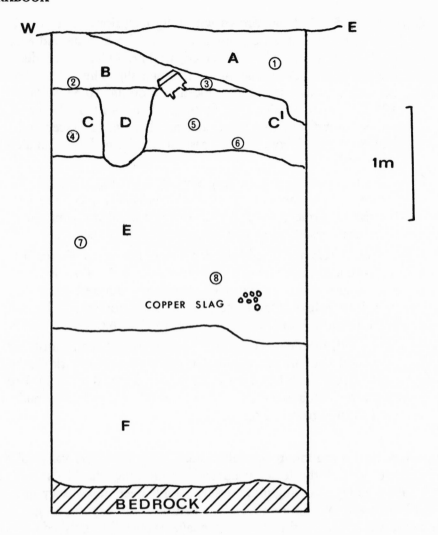

**Figure 10.4.** North wall of the sondage at Rong Numba showing the bronze vessel embedded in the face. The positions of charcoal samples (①–⑧) are projected.

**TABLE 10.1.  Rong Numba: radiocarbon dates**

| LOCATION (see fig. 10.4) | LEVEL | LAB. # | DATE |
|---|---|---|---|
| 1 | A | NBg–4875 | 800 ± 60 A.D. |
| 2 | B | NBg–4876 | 550 ± 120 B.C. |
| 3 | B | AoK–9561 | 280 ± 70 B.C. |
| 4 | C | NBg–4877 | 800 ± 180 B.C. |
| 5 | C' | NBg–4878 | 1800 ± 200 B.C. |
| 6 | C' | AoK–9562 | 350 ± 100 B.C. |
| 7 | E | NBg–4879 | 2500 ± 210 B.C. |
| 8 | E | AoK–9563 | 400 ± 150 B.C. |

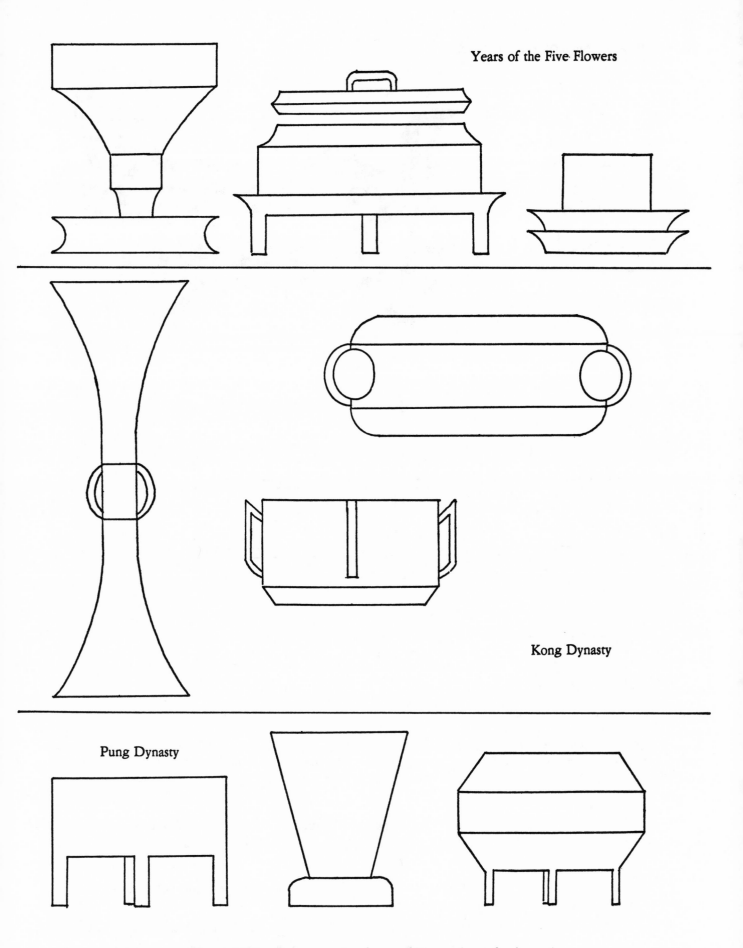

Years of the Five Flowers

Kong Dynasty

Pung Dynasty

Figure 10.5.  Representative forms of Kwangchung food vessels

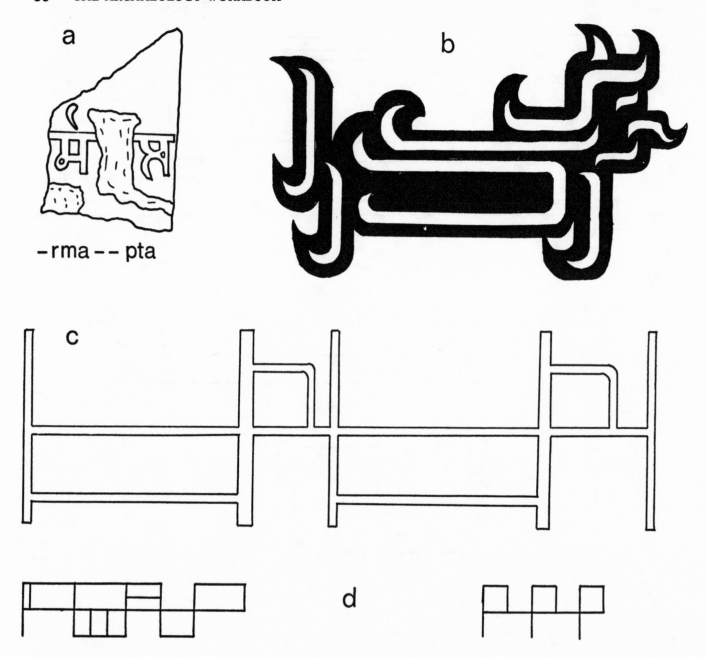

-rma - - pta

**Figure 10.6.** Tablet fragment (a) from Tai Pin, layer B, with transliteration, and (b–d) motifs from Kwangchung and Ankang art; (b) *si mai tung* motif of the Years of the Five Flowers; (c) detail of decoration on Lon Gon bronze no. 4; (d) typical geometric designs of early Pung Dynasty pottery

varieties of pepper, bean, and cucurbit resembling the modern cultivars of the region, whose wild ancestors no longer exist.

**SCHOLARLY REACTION:** Typical of scholarly reaction following on the publication of these results are the following excerpts:

It is gratifying that archaeological evidence should so strikingly confirm the historical reality of the extension of southern Kwangchung influence into the outlying region of Ankang during the Years of the Five Flowers. It is now clear that the corpus of Lon Gon bronzes represents a crude and unsophisticated imitation of the contemporary Kwangchung forms, borrowing thence the tripod form but not the flanged platforms that give such elegant repose to the food vessels of the Years of the Five Flowers [cf. fig. 10.5]. Another devolved feature can be seen in the decoration on the side of one of the Tai Pin vessels. Here the *si mai tung* or "running dog" motif of contemporary Kwangchung bronzework has become a frieze of simple rectilinear lines [cf. fig. 10.6:b & c]. It is almost certainly to southern Kwangchung influence, also, that we should attribute the pre-Dharmagupta stone-built city which appears to have arisen at the site of Tai Pin by about 400 B.C.

> Sir Cedric Gardewycket, Emeritus
> Keeper of Ancient Sinology at the
> King's Waterfield Museum, Berkshire,
> in his Presidential Address to the
> Royal Society of Asian Antiquarians

These findings throw the strongest doubt on the place of Kwangchung as a cradle of East Asian civilization. With the establishment of copper-working in Ankang during the third millennium B.C., and of food production long before that, it now seems likely that developmental influences can be traced from Ankang to Kwangchung. The Lon Gon bronzes are dated, by associated pottery and isotopic analyses, to around 2000 B.C. Their severe classicism can be seen to give rise to the more restrained Kwangchung food vessels of the early Pung Dynasty, before the Kwangchung tradition became debased by overelaboration and virtuoso indulgence. It is noteworthy that exactly the same decorative approach is used on the decorated Tai Pin vessel and on the Kwangchung incised ceramics of the early Pung [cf. fig 10.6:c, d & e]. Perhaps at last Ankang will be granted rightful recognition as a cultural and artistic fountainhead in eastern Asia.

> Dr. Clint P. Trailblazer, Associate
> Professor, Department of the History
> of Art, Multnomah State University,
> New Frisia, in *Art Frontier,* II (1986)

Notwithstanding the advances that have come about with the application of quantitative methods to archaeology, the student still has to weigh evidence as well as to count it. Above all, he or she must learn, while retaining respect for the eminent, to go to the data and not merely to the "authorities." How then do *you* read the story of Kwangchung-Ankang relations?

# PROBLEM 11 | The Kurgans of Nalevo

The following is taken from A. L. L. Bezaroff's seminal work *The Materialist Conception of History Applied to the Soviet Past* (Moscow, 1949):

The Nalevo region lies north of the Sea of Azov. The interfluvial zone, 200–500 meters above sea level and with degraded *chernozem* (black prairie) soils, was intensively occupied during the Neolithic, Chalcolithic, and Bronze Ages, as is known by the large numbers of kurgans (burial mounds or barrows) found in this part of the region (fig. 11.1). On the other hand, the marshes and *solod* (black alkali) soils remained virtually uninhabited throughout this period. Until the recent reclamation of the *solod* by Nalevo agricultural collectives, forest, dominated by alder, willow, and oak, grew on either side of the riverine marshes. The steppic vegetation of the *chernozems* is characterized by herbaceous plants and rare relict stands of beech and ash.

The kurgans and unique Cherlok earthwork attracted antiquarian interest throughout the nineteenth century, landowners often ordering their serfs to open up a kurgan for the amusement of guests down for the wildfowling. This casual plundering of our national heritage led to no serious publications but merely dilletantish notes and sketches appearing in the bourgeois idealist journals of the pre-Revolutionary period. In the 1920s a group of Young Communists, who had spontaneously formed themselves into an archaeological society, mapped the kurgans in surveys later published by S. T. Alkienko (1931), and after the Great Fatherland War (1941–45), a team from the Academy of Sciences of the USSR undertook the first and so far only scientific excavations in the region.

I shall first summarize the archaeological findings by period and then elucidate the evolution of the family and of the relations of production.

## THE NEOLITHIC

Low kurgans up to sixty-eight meters long and two meters high are typical of the Neolithic. The Marpolchik site excavated by the academy may serve as an example. This kurgan was built up by a succession of burials, each in a shallow pit over which earth was heaped in such a way as to make every new mound an extension of those covering earlier burials. This process of accretionary growth, while unrecognized previously as such, appears from nineteenth-century comments to be diagnostic of Neolithic kurgans. Similarly

88

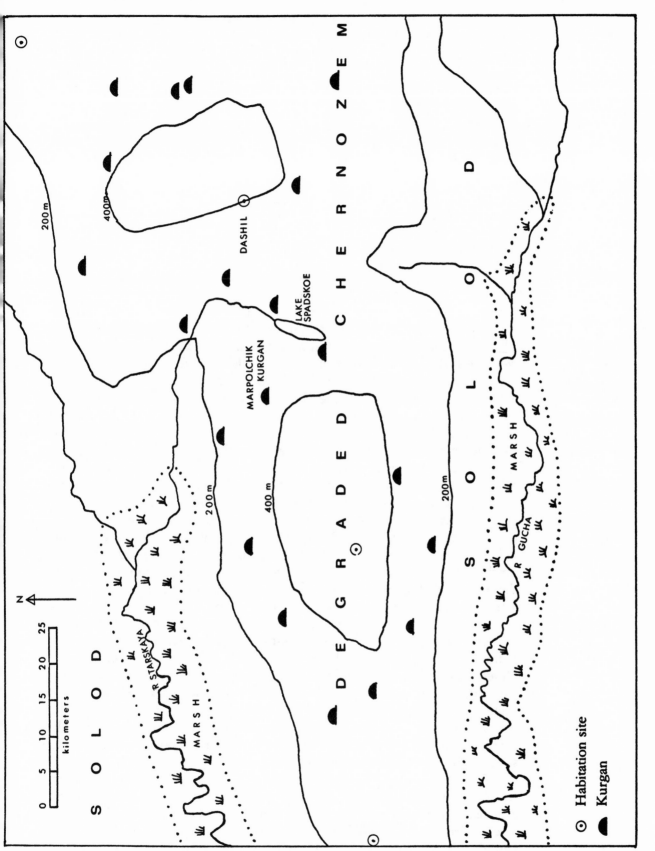

**Figure 11.1.** The Nalevo region showing soils and the distributions of Neolithic habitation sites and kurgans (after Bezaroff, 1949)

**TABLE 11.1.  Burials and gravegoods from the Marpolchik kurgan**

|  | ADULTS | | JUVENILES | INFANTS |
|  | MALES | FEMALES | JUVENILES | INFANTS |
|---|---|---|---|---|
| Numbers | 32 | 27 | 43 | 71 |
| Gravegoods |  |  |  |  |
| Plaques | 173 | 84 | 106 | 140 |
| Shell beads | 153 | 276 | 220 | 98 |
| Flint tools | 66 | 35 | 21 | 5 |
| Pots | 38 | 52 | 81 | 91 |
| Figurines | — | 27 | 5 | — |
| Maceheads | 5 | — | — | — |
| Copper knife | 1 | — | — | — |
| Exotic beads | 55 | 26 | 2 | — |

the grave furniture found here can be duplicated in the formerly private collections now assembled in the Marlova Museum of Soviet Progress (table 11.1). The dead were buried wearing garments, long since decayed, to which were sewn shell beads and plaques made of laminae from boars' tusks. The plaques were carved to depict cattle (396 examples), deer (98), wild boar (5), and snakes (4). The burials are also accompanied by flint tools, including knives, scrapers, and arrowheads, and conical-based examples of the typical cord-marked Neolithic pottery of the region. Rarer items include female figurines in baked clay, a copper knife, and maceheads (one of which had been carefully repaired) made of porphyry from the Ural Mountains, 1,000 kilometers to the northeast, and a number of beads made of marble and rock crystal from the Caucasus Mountains, 500 kilometers to the south.

Besides various dispersed scatters of Neolithic pottery, four sites of this period have been recognized (fig. 11.1), but only one, the large Dashil village, has as yet been investigated by the academy. The site, 20 kilometers northeast of Lake Spadskoe, covers some 4 hectares. Excavations over half of the site revealed the remains of 2 large and several small timber-built houses. There is abundant evidence of agriculture in the form of grindstones and storage pits. The pottery, like that from the kurgans, is decorated with cord impressions but usually flat based. Flat-based painted wares are also present in the two large houses, and these also produced numbers of copper artifacts. Other small finds included a wide range of flint tools, including axes, hoes, and arrowheads, numerous beads, many in exotic stones, and quantities of fragmentary plaques representing (in descending order of frequency) *Sus, Bos,* snakes, and deer. The animal bone from the site has not yet been fully analyzed, but it is known that all of these animals are represented except the snakes. The microfauna includes large numbers of rats and mice.

The most remarkable discovery made at Dashil was of a well or cistern (the uppermost parts of which had been destroyed by erosion) containing the articulated skeletons of no less than 23 men, women, and children (fig. 11.2). The children's bones show evidence of severe rickets, but there are no other pathological features. The coarse sand and gravel overlying the bone bed contains a few typically Dashil artifacts.

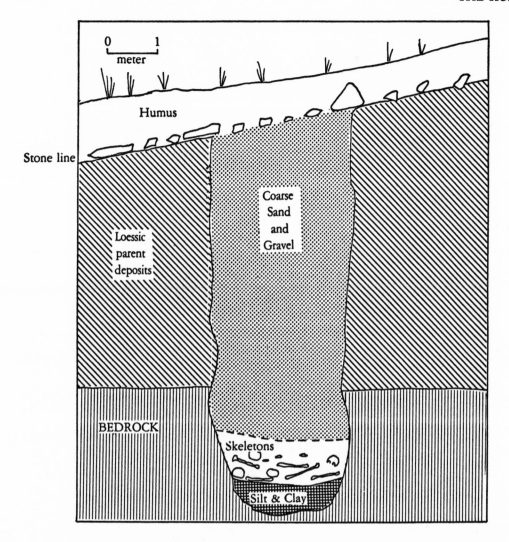

Figure 11.2.   The Dashil wellshaft: section

## THE CHALCOLITHIC (figure 11.3)

The kurgans of this period are quite different from those of the Neolithic, being round, up to 6 meters in height, and containing the remains of two- or three-roomed timber structures supported by large boulders. Each room is occupied by a single burial, usually of an adult male, very rarely of a juvenile, splendidly furnished with grave goods. Axe-adzes and daggers of copper are common, together with beads of gold, silver, copper, and exotic stones imported from the Urals and the Caucasus. Boars' tusk plaques depict the same range of species present at Dashil. Beside each corpse was deposited a flat-based painted vase.

Secondary inhumations without or with few and undiagnostic grave goods are commonly found dug shallowly into the surface of Chalcolithic kurgans.

When villages of this period have been identified, they will no doubt provide abundant evidence of the economic developments that characterize

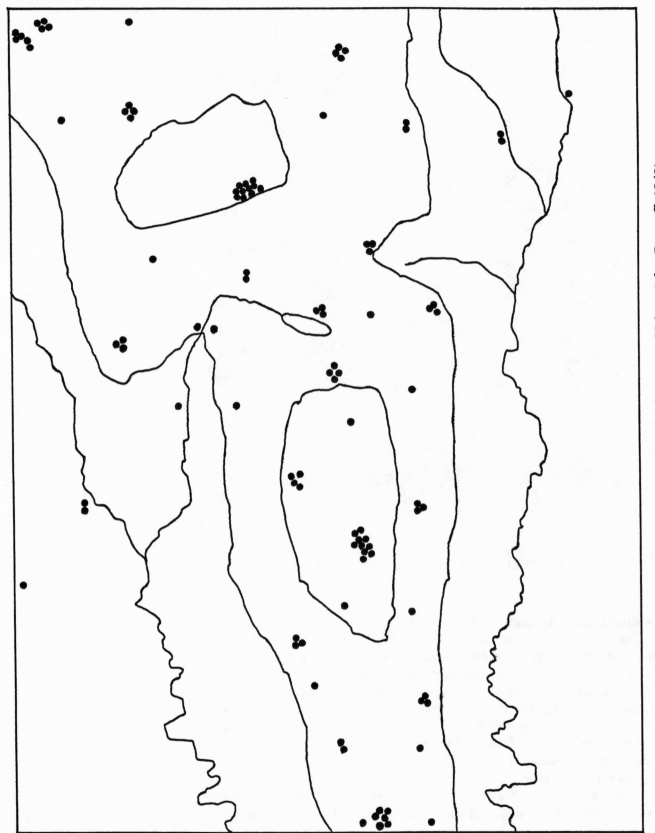

Figure 11.3.    The distribution of Chalcolithic kurgans in Nalevo (after Bezaroff, 1949)

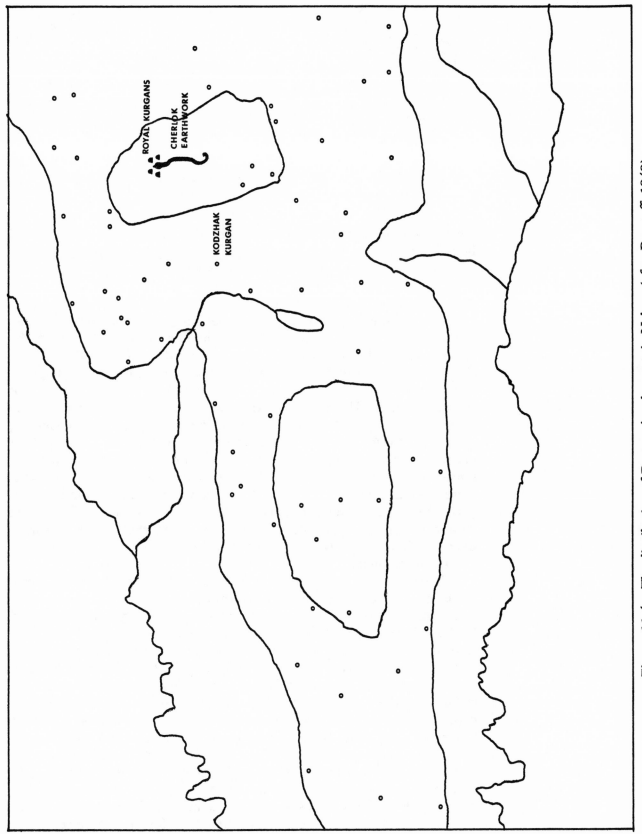

ROYAL KURGANS

CHERLOK
EARTHWORK

○ KODZHAK
KURGAN

Figure 11.4. The distribution of Bronze Age kurgans in Nalevo (after Bezaroff, 1949)

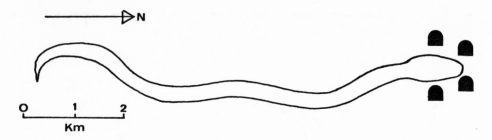

Figure 11.5.   The Cherlok earthwork and associated "Royal Kurgans"

the Chalcolithic. A degree of cultural continuity is, however, demonstrated by some of the grave furniture and by the archaizing tendency for the largest kurgan clusters to be located near major Neolithic sites.

**THE BRONZE AGE (figure 11.4)**

Bronze Age kurgans tend to be rather smaller than those of the Chalcolithic. In stone cists located on the original ground surface beneath the barrows, pairs of burials are often found in which the wife was killed and laid beside her husband. Bronze tools and weapons are usually present together with pectoral ornaments of bone or bronze depicting mythical animals, half snake, half cattle. There is wide variation in the richness of the remaining grave goods; only about 10 percent of the kurgans contain gold ornaments, most have at least one or two beads of exotic stone, and all contain at least one pottery vessel decorated with bands of herringbone motifs and containing horse bones from the funerary sacrifice. In a small proportion of instances, there is clear evidence of craft specialization. For example, the Kodzhak kurgan [which interestingly had been built in an area that had previously been plowed, see fig. 11.7] contained the remains of a man who from the associated tools must have been a weaver. He could not afford, it would seem, much in the way of ornament.

In striking contrast to all but the richest barrows are the so-called Royal Kurgans associated with the Cherlok earthwork (fig. 11.5). This monumental structure, 8 kilometers long and about 7 meters high, was movingly described by Alkienko as "representing on a vast and magnificent scale the composite warrior's bow so typical of our native steppes. . . . a gesture of defiance hurled through the ages into the faces of our enemies." The Royal Kurgans, of which there are four, each contain a single adult male skeleton laid in a beechwood coffin embellished with relief carvings of horses and snakes. The coffins were deposited in deep chambered pits or catacombs filled with gold and silver bowls and finely made Bronze Age pottery vessels containing smaller ornaments of precious metals and other imported items. The entrance to the catacomb is in all four cases guarded by the skeleton of an exceptionally large bull. In the midst of all this wealth, the bodies of the kings were placed in their coffins unadorned save for a silver diadem composed of intertwined serpents. The Royal Kurgans are the only ones regularly found to have secondary inhumations; these are otherwise rare.

It is unfortunate that although scatters of Bronze Age herringbone pottery turn up here and there all over the interfluvial zone, Soviet archaeologists have thus far been unable to identify the capital city of Bronze Age Nalevo.

## DEVELOPMENT OF THE FAMILY AND OF THE PRODUCTIVE FORCES

The Nalevo sequence exhibits the classic developmental patterns unerringly delineated by F. Engels (1884) in *The Origin of the Family, Private Property, and the State.* The Neolithic peoples, at the lower stage of barbarism, were cultivators of plants and breeders of cattle. The distribution of kurgans—each in the center of its clan or gentile lands—the communal burials, and the female figurines associated with the women are ample proof of an undifferentiated clan society characterized by mother right. Human labor yielded little surplus over the cost of its maintenance.

Toward the end of the Neolithic period, however, increases in cattle breeding and external relations created entirely new social relationships. Private property in herds must have developed at an early stage and, according to the division of labor then prevailing, ownership of this wealth would have accrued to the men. As the family did not increase as rapidly as cattle, extra herdsmen and milkmaids became necessary. Labor power thus acquired an exchange value, and slavery was invented. The Chalcolithic kurgans with their richly adorned male burials and secondary (slave) inhumations show that the matriarchal gens had by now given way to the patriarchal, slave-owning clan. That this revolution, one of the most decisive ever experienced by man, was not achieved without bloodshed, is indicated by the Dashil wellshaft massacre.

With the Bronze Age we arrive at the stage of upper barbarism; the dialectic of history has led to a more complex division of labor and to the pairing, monogamian family. In order to guarantee the paternity of the children, the woman is placed in man's absolute power; if he kills her, or if she is murdered at his death, he is but exercising his social right. Therefore we find kurgans containing monogamous couples as the primary burials. The variable richness of grave furniture demonstrates that class antagonism has sprung up, making necessary the creation of a power standing above society, that of the state, personified in Nalevo by the kings entombed in the Royal Kurgans.

Further elaboration is unnecessary except to note that there can be no better demonstration of the power of the objective materialist interpretation of history than its successful application to data gathered in large part by the entrepreneurial clericalist archaeologists of Tsarist Russia. (*end of extract*)

**NEW DATA:**

At the time Bezaroff was writing, radiocarbon dating did not exist. His chronology is therefore relative and based primarily upon the pottery. The museum collections have, however, now provided samples for dating with the results set out in table 11.2. Pollen spectra have been obtained from the coring of Lake Spadskoe and the rate of deposition calibrated by radiocarbon dates (fig. 11.6). Another sample scraped from the interior of a Dashil pot shows a pollen spectrum consisting of 32% arboreal pollen and 68% nonarboreal pollen, of which approximately half is made up of wheat, barley, and

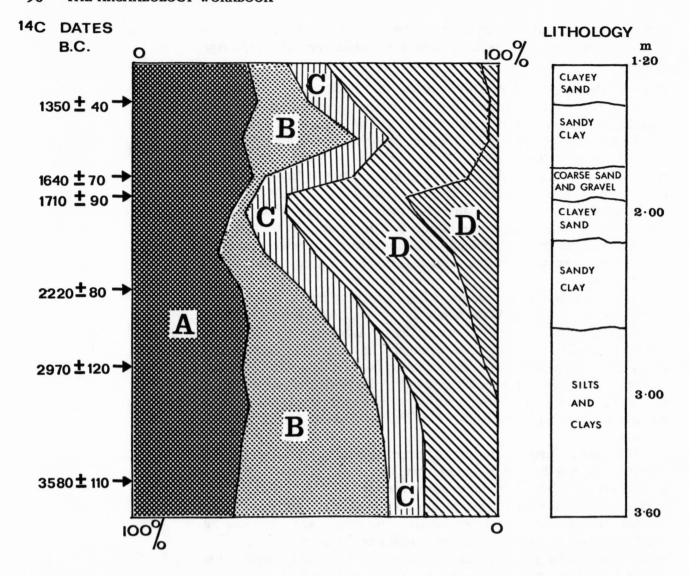

**Figure 11.6.** Simplified pollen diagram of part of the Lake Spadskoe core showing floral associations (A-D), radiocarbon dates and core lithology

**Key to Floral Associations:** A: Oak, alder, and willow association typical of wetter soils; B: Beech and ash association characteristic of drier soils; C: Reeds and sedges typical of marshy environments; D: Herbaceous plants (grasses, clovers, etc.) characteristic of steppe (D': Cereal, *Triticum* and *Hordeum,* cultivars)

**TABLE 11.2.  Radiocarbon dates from Nalevo sites**

| LAB. # | DATE | SAMPLE MATERIAL AND PROVENIENCE |
|---|---|---|
| MOS–4326 | 2575 + 100 B.C. | Human bone from the Marpolchik kurgan |
| MOS–4327 | 1800 + 60 B.C. | Timber from a house at Dashil |
| MOS–4328 | 2860 + 110 B.C. | Human bone from a Neolithic kurgan |
| MOS–4329 | 1860 + 100 B.C. | Human bone from a Chalcolithic kurgan |
| MOS–4330 | 1510 + 50 B.C. | Wood from a "Royal Kurgan" coffin |
| MOS–4331 | 1430 + 40 B.C. | Cattle bone from the Kodzhak kurgan |

weeds of cultivation. Third, aerial photography has revealed the presence of prehistoric field systems. These formerly covered most of the interfluvial zone but have been largely obscured by an erosional episode that, in the view of a senior Soviet geomorphologist, may well have been precipitated by overexploitation of the *chernozems*. An area in which the field system is relatively well preserved is illustrated in Figure 11.7.

You are now invited to restudy Bezaroff's data in the light of these new sources of information and to consider whether his attribution of sites to phases is correct and whether his interpretation of socioeconomic development requires modification.

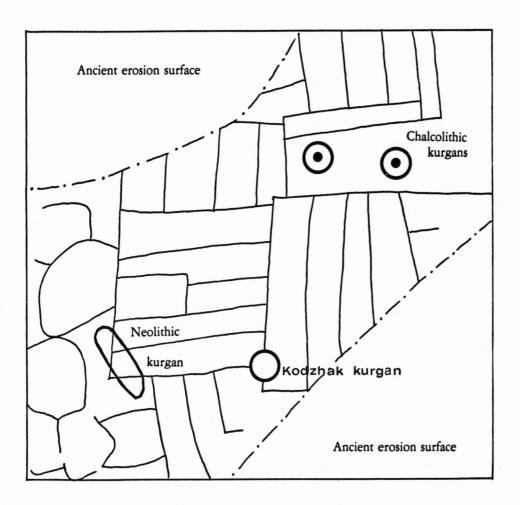

**Figure 11.7.** Field systems revealed by aerial photography

# The Cemetery of Bilj

**BACKGROUND
INFORMATION:**

The Ruritanian Hač Mountains, sometimes called the "cockpit of the Balkans," have throughout history been a cultural backwater into which ideas filtered only slowly. Their picturesque inhabitants (see *International Geographical Magazine,* No. 769) are the descendants of the many refugee populations who, in flight before invaders of the lowland plains, have sought sanctuary in the hills. So it was in prehistory. In a little-known fragment of his *Ges Periodos* (A Voyage Around the World), Hekataios (*fl.* 500 B.C.), the "grandfather of history," described the situation as it must have existed some two generations before his time:

> The Chroesnes mountains [as they were known to the Greeks] are inhabited by two tribes, the Botachoi and the Iardames, who having been much harried by raids of the riders from the steppes north of the Euxine [Black] Sea there live in perfect amity one with another. Alone among barbarians these peoples are said to worship the setting Sun and to abhor rosy-fingered Dawn.

**ARCHAEO-
LOGICAL DATA:**

Dr. Matlo, an enthusiastic amateur prehistorian and man of letters, discovered and excavated a cemetery at Bilj, a small village below the provincial town of Foksul. He found a total of 20 graves, 6 of which contained cremations in urns. He has published a short paper containing a list of grave furniture (table 12.1), drawings of a number of finds (figure 12.1), and a plan (figure 12.2). The plan is semischematic and shows the urns in cross section with the cremated remains (including artifacts burned with the body) represented *inside* the urns, and any other grave goods depicted outside as they were found in the pit containing the urn. He noted that bones were very poorly preserved; only in a few cases was it possible to determine the sex or other physical characteristics of the burials.

Dr. Matlo attributes the cemetery to the transition between the Bronze and Iron Ages, which he was here able to date to the first half of the sixth century B.C. on the evidence of a Cimmerian horse bridle bit of the late seventh century (Grave 7) and a Scythian horse cheek piece of the sixth century (Grave 20). Although he suggested that the cemetery may have served a village occupied by both Botachoi and Iardames, Dr. Matlo made no attempt to place the burials in chronological order and did not assign individuals to one or the other ethnic group. Nor, except on the basis of the fragmentary biological evidence, did he try to determine their ages, sexes,

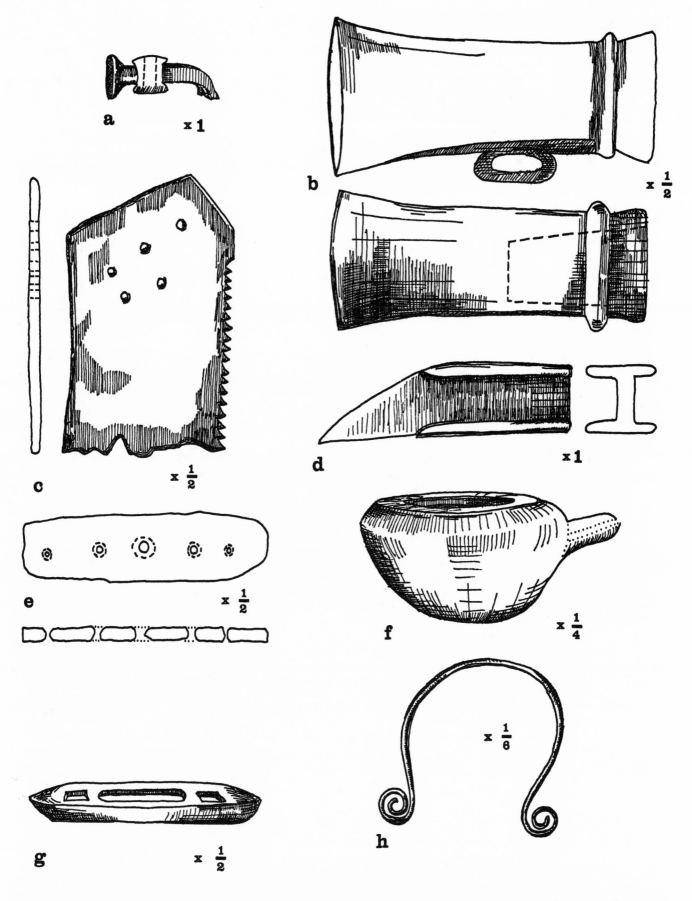

**Figure 12.1.** Artifacts from Bilj Cemetery: a: shaft-hole hammer; b: socketed hammer; c: saw fragment; d: flanged adze; e: pierced metal plate; f: hollow-spouted bowl; g: bone shuttle; h: gold torc. Scales indicated

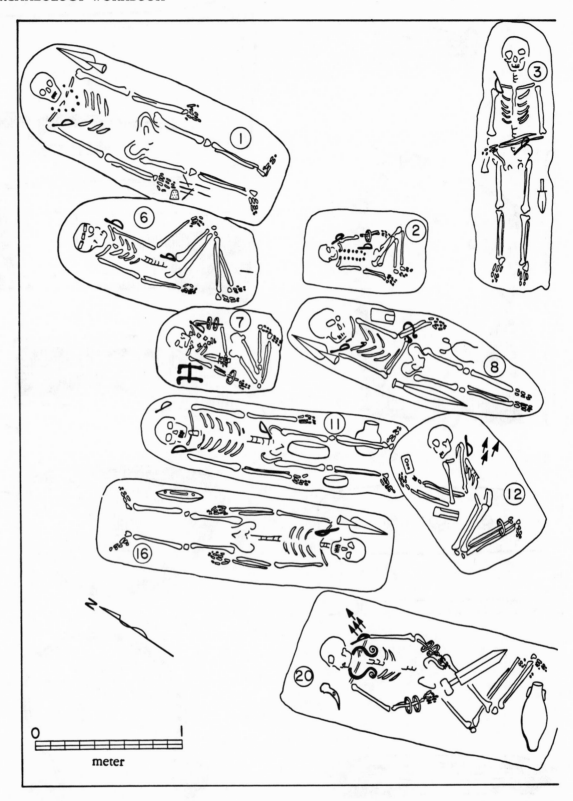

**Figure 12.2.**  Bilj Cemetery: plan showing burials and associated grave furniture (see *Key*)

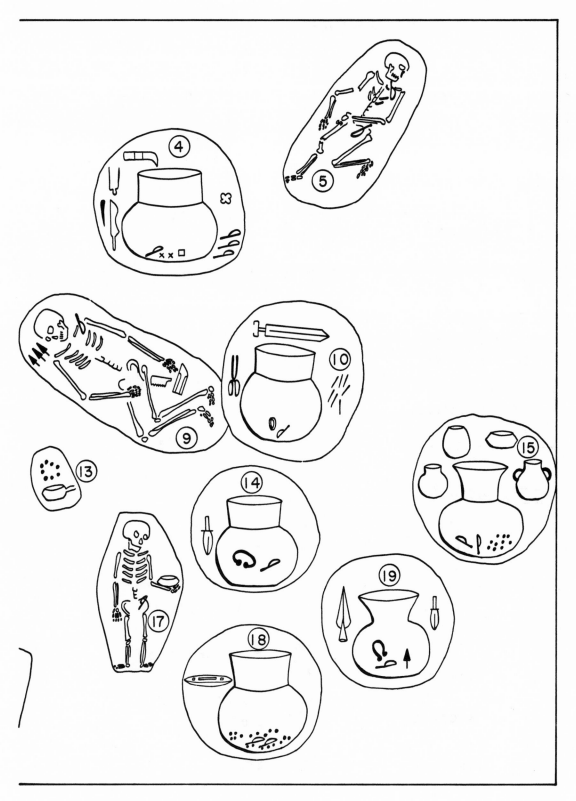

# KEY TO ARTIFACTS

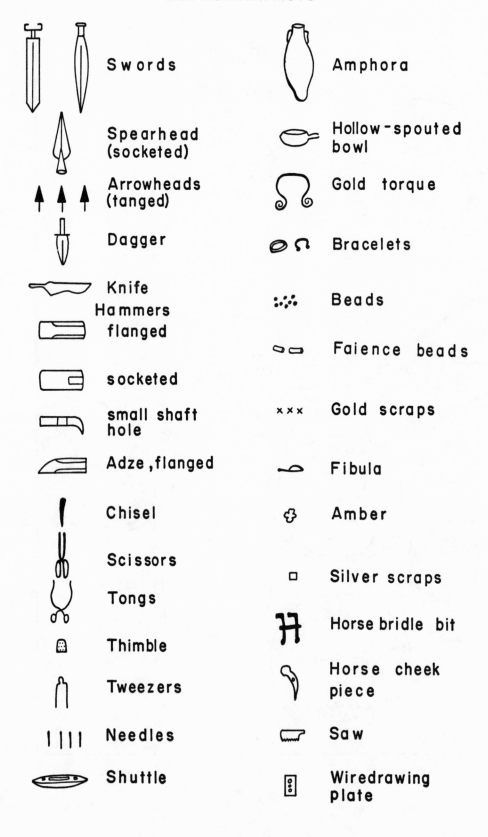

| | |
|---|---|
| Swords | Amphora |
| Spearhead (socketed) | Hollow-spouted bowl |
| Arrowheads (tanged) | Gold torque |
| Dagger | Bracelets |
| Knife | Beads |
| Hammers flanged | Faience beads |
| socketed | Gold scraps |
| small shaft hole | Fibula |
| Adze, flanged | Amber |
| Chisel | Silver scraps |
| Scissors | Horse bridle bit |
| Tongs | Horse cheek piece |
| Thimble | |
| Tweezers | Saw |
| Needles | Wiredrawing plate |
| Shuttle | |

**TABLE 12.1.** The graves and their contents (All artifacts are of copper or bronze unless otherwise stated)

| GRAVE NO. | BURIAL TYPE | SEX | WEAPONS | TOOLS, ETC. | ORNAMENTS | REMARKS |
|---|---|---|---|---|---|---|
| 1 | Extended | ? | Socketed spearhead | Thimble 14 needles | Stone beads Fibula | |
| 2 | Flexed | F | — | — | Beads Bracelet 2 fibulae | |
| 3 | Extended | ? | Dagger | — | 2 fibulae | Right hand severed some time before death, wound healed and bony regrowth |
| 4 | Urn | ? | Knife | Small shaft-hole hammer (fig. 12.1a) Fine chisel Tweezers | 2 scraps of gold sheet 1 lump silver 1 piece amber 4 fibulae | |
| 5 | ? | F | — | — | 2 fibulae | Skull fractured and several bones broken *ad mortem* |
| 6 | Flexed | ? | — | Needle | 2 fibulae Faience beads | Arthritic lesions of lumbar vertebrae |
| 7 | Flexed | ? | Dagger | Horse bridle bit | 3 bracelets Amber beads Fibula | Sagittal suture of skull unfused |
| 8 | Extended | ? | Socketed spearhead Sword | Socketed hammer (fig. 12.1b) Tongs | Bracelet Fibula | |
| 9 | Flexed | ? | 12 arrowheads | Saw fragment (fig. 12.1c) Flanged adze (fig. 12.1d) | Fibula | |
| 10 | Urn | M | Sword | Scissors 13 needles | Fibula Bracelet | |
| 11 | Extended | ? | — | 3 pots | 3 fibulae | |
| 12 | Flexed | ? | 7 arrowheads | Flanged hammer Pierced metal plate (fig. 12.1e) | Bracelet Fibula | |
| 13 | ? | ? | — | Bowl with hollow spout (fig. 12.1f) | Beads | No bones preserved |
| 14 | Urn | ? | Dagger | — | Bracelet Fibula | |
| 15 | Urn | F | — | 4 pots | Iron beads 2 fibulae | |
| 16 | Extended | M | Socketed spearhead | Bone shuttle (fig. 12.1g) | Fibula | |
| 17 | Extended | ? | — | Bowl | Fibula | Trunk:limb proportions suggest achondroplasia |
| 18 | Urn | ? | — | Bone shuttle | Beads Fibulae | |
| 19 | Urn | ? | Iron dagger Socketed spearhead Arrowhead | — | Fibula Bracelet | |
| 20 | Flexed | ? | Sword 18 arrowheads | Horse cheekpiece | Gold torc (fig. 12.1h) 4 silver bracelets Fibula Amphora | Traces of timber present around sides of grave |

craft, or other occupations or social status. His paper ends with a quote from Sir Thomas Browne's *Hydriotaphia, Urne Buriall:*

> What song the *Syrens* sang, or what name *Achilles* assumed when he hid himself among women, though puzling Questions are not beyond all conjecture. What time the persons of these Ossuaries entred the famous Nations of the dead, and slept with Princes and Counsellours, might admit a wide solution. But who were the proprietaries of these bones, or what bodies these ashes made up, were a question above Antiquarism.*

Do you agree? After all, the contingency table below suggests that there may be many significant associations requiring interpretation.

| | NUMBER OF FIBULAE | |
|---|---|---|
| | ONE | MORE THAN ONE |
| PRESENT WEAPONS (incl. daggers, knives) | 10 | 2 |
| ABSENT | 1 | 6 |

---

*Sir Thomas Browne, *Urne Buriall and the Garden of Cyrus,* ed. John Carter (Cambridge: Cambridge University Press, 1958), p. 44.

# Indians and Europeans in Early Colonial New Frisia

The state of New Frisia lies on the Gulf of Mexico between Florida and Alabama (figure 13.1). The first colonizers were Spanish conquistadors under the captaincy of El Verso Blunt, an English renegade in the service of King Philip. In 1559 they founded a settlement, La Insular, on an island in a lagoon at the mouth of the Rio Partagas. This was to be their base for exploitation of the fabled, and indeed fabulous, gold of the interior. In 1571 a boatload of Dutch colonists from the Spanish Netherlands, members of a Catabaptist sect fleeing from the persecutions of the Duke of Alva, landed 120 kilometers to the east and began their highly successful penetration of the interior, reaching the upper Partagas some 60 years later.

In its early days, La Insular failed to prosper; the promised gold had proved illusory, and the pearls, furs, and skins obtained from the natives did not justify the high cost of transport between Nueva Estremadura (as the Spanish had baptized the territory) and metropolitan Spain. Capitan de Tueros, Blunt's successor, was recommending abandonment when, in 1588, the town received the visit of Fr. Arturo Fuente, a Jesuit agent of the Inquisition. Besides searching out heresy in all its forms and chastising the inhabitants for their lack of moral fiber, Fuente proved a good businessman, advocating the establishment of a tobacco plantation and factory. From 1596 the tobaccos and cigars of Nueva Estremadura began to enjoy a reputation in Spain and financed renewed attempts to forge more profitable trading links with the Macanudo Indians living higher up the Rio Partagas and along its tributaries. However, after initial successes, the Spanish came into conflict with the Dutch, who in 1633 made a lightning campaign down the river and razed La Insular to the ground, thus putting an end to Spanish ambitions on this part of the Gulf Coast.

*from* H. Winterman, *The Early History of New Frisia*

Helena Larga reviewed Winterman's book in the *Journal of Precolonial Studies,* severely criticizing its author as

. . . totally Europocentric. We learn nothing of the Macanudo Indians who still form 26% of the population of the state, nor of their relations with their unwelcome guests. The *History* is inadequate even in its own terms. Why, for example, should the Spanish colonists have failed in spite of their profit-making commercial enterprise and strong support from the homeland? How did the Dutch manage to push forward their frontier into pre-

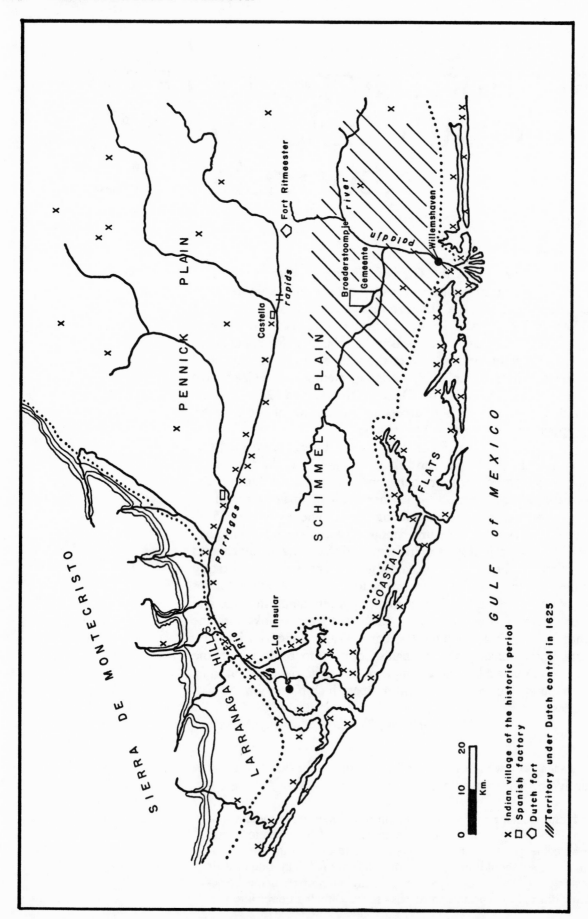

Figure 13.1.  New Frisia in the early seventeenth century

× Indian village of the historic period
□ Spanish factory
◇ Dutch fort
/// Territory under Dutch control in 1625

sumably hostile Indian territory, while the Spaniards remained confined to the Rio Partagas?

In the next issue of the *Journal,* Winterman replied, stating that

A historian is constrained by his sources, and in this instance, with the exception of Fr. Fuente's report, the Spanish documents consist almost entirely of requests for equipment and supplies, commercial statements and the like. On the Dutch side the situation is, if anything, worse, though we do have an interesting map in the form of a sampler embroidered by Hanna Upman showing the Broederstroompje Gemeente (community) as it was in 1608 (figure 13.2). The large numbers of Catabaptist tracts make little or no mention of Indians, saving those who had entered into their service, and here the Dutch concern was rather with their souls than with ethnographic description of their life-ways.

I have nonetheless combed the sources and come up with the information given in the Appendix to this reply. The reader will note that while it is of some curiosity value, it does not go far towards answering Ms. Larga's questions nor resolve what I concede to be genuine historical issues. Perhaps archaeology can help.

## THE APPENDIX TO WINTERMAN'S REPLY

(*Editor's note:* The majority of the following quotations are taken from *A True Relation of the Maine Land of Nueva Estremadura, beeing Part of Florida, and of the Nature and Disposition of her Inhabitants,* by A. Fidalgo of Havana, 1568. References are omitted for reasons of space.)

. . . The savages are tawny like an olive and goe naked saving a clout of hide wherewith they cover their privities. Their skins are painted by the prycking in of soot in divers designs as each to his fancy deviseth. . . .

When younge their heads are so bound about against a board that their browes are flattened and in such a wise that the Christans first beholding them believed them not men but Devils. . . .

The Indians are wel proportioned but thievish, subtil and vain. Men and women hang themselves about with certaine trifles, jewels and bracelets of shell and of a stone called mica that shineth exceedingly. This is their looking glasse that the women greatly covet passing many hours before to binde up their haire in pleits in severall manner. The women have a round piece of shell hanging at their eares like a Calicut Die; they are wel-favoured to behold
. . . .

Their Caciques and Counsellours have much estimation of copper wrought flat and graven which they wear upon their breasts and foreheads
. . . .

Of religion have they none but worshippe the Sunne and the Devil. In each towne is a temple upon a high mount made for defense whereon sitteth the likeness of a great bird or eagle. The priestes devine what shall come to pass whether good or evil casting stones graven with magick signs of beestes or an eye weeping. . . .

The cotages are of timber with sides of clay and covered with thatch withal. Grain is kept in a *barbacoa,* neere adjoyning, that is a room raised on four poles. . . .

Their victuals are fish and tortugas and shell whereof there is great plenty but satisfyeth not. They make pottage of a graine the bigness of a pease, the

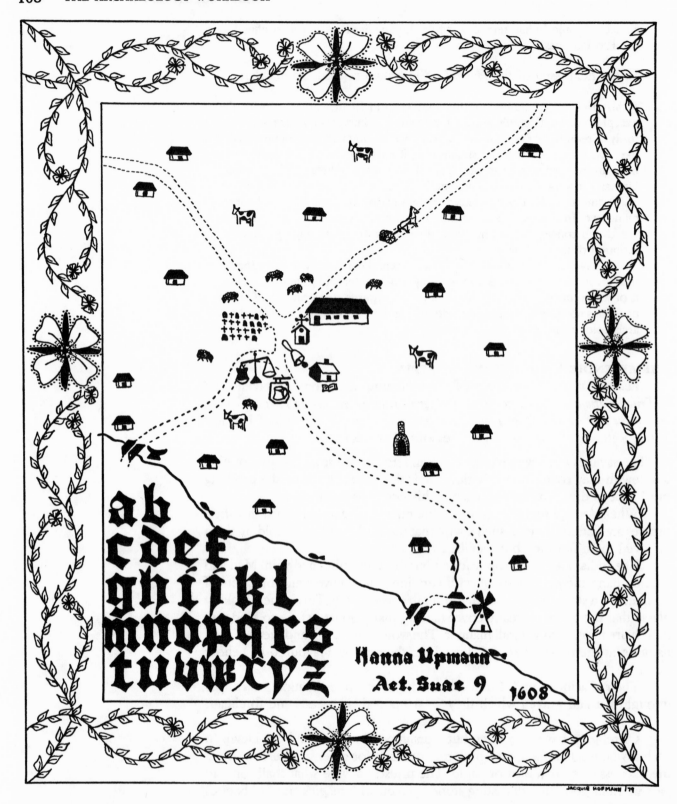

**Figure 13.2.**  The Upmann sampler, showing the Broederstroompje Gemeente as it was in 1608. Historical research suggests the interpretation of the symbols given on the facing page:

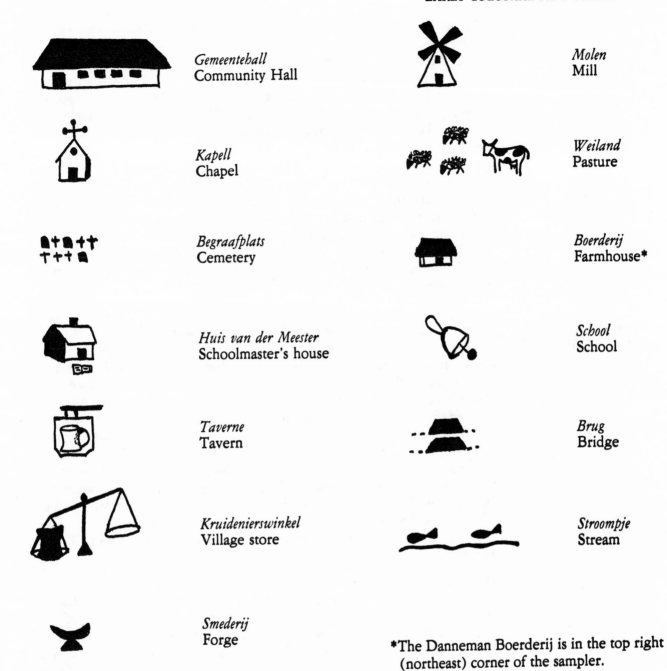

Gemeentehall
Community Hall

Molen
Mill

Kapell
Chapel

Weiland
Pasture

Begraafplats
Cemetery

Boerderij
Farmhouse*

Huis van der Meester
Schoolmaster's house

School
School

Taverne
Tavern

Brug
Bridge

Kruidenierswinkel
Village store

Stroompje
Stream

Smederij
Forge

*The Danneman Boerderij is in the top right (northeast) corner of the sampler.

Stenenbakkerij
Brickworks

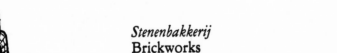

ear whereof is like unto a teasel. They also have faire pumpions and beanes. Grapes and a fruit called *ameixas* they gather in the thickets. . . .

The women doe all the businesse at home, make vessels of clay and paniers of palme leaves. They plant with an instrument that is the shoulder of a bul fashioned like a mattocke. They sew cloakes of their flax and of feathers and paint the hides of staggages and hindes the men having dressed them according to their custome. . . .

Of beastes there are cattel, deer, foxes, cunnies, ounces, leopards and unicorns. They have no herds but turkeycockes and small dogges which is an excellent meate. . . .

The men when they be not at warre pass their days in fishing from weirs or with nets and in hunting. Their weapons are bows and arrows of cane pointed with a bone of fish, others with a stone like point of diamond. Javelings have they also of horne of stagge. They are cunning to make their houses and canoas with adzes of a great shell for they have no metall in that countrye save copper and a little silver. They fashion stone right well and carve wood with a chysel that is the tooth of a mighty fish. . . .

Each of them bare a drumme in their hand or a flute and so entered dancing and singing in lamentable tune upon their festival. After the sacrifice of blood they buried him as is their custome garlanded about with pearls and heaped up a mound of sand to his memorial. . . .

The men have a kind of herb dried, who with a cup of earth or of stone carved in effigie if they bee warriors or ancients with fire they suck up the smoke thereof. . . .

## HISTORICAL ARCHAEOLOGY:

Due to the large numbers of New Frisian citizens who claim ancestors among the first Dutch settlers or who are of mixed Spanish and Indian descent, there is considerable local interest in historical archaeology. Indian village sites of the late sixteenth and early seventeenth century have been identified if not exhaustively surveyed (see fig. 13.1), and the site of La Insular has been planned (figure 13.3). Limited excavations have taken place at La Insular and, on the upper Rio Partagas, at the Castella site, which combines a Spanish factory or trading post and an Indian village. Two early Dutch sites have also been dug: one in the Broederstroompje community is a Boerderij (farmstead) that belonged to the Danneman family and was abandoned after a pneumonia epidemic in 1610; the other is an isolated redoubt, Fort Ritmeester, on a hill overlooking the Partagas valley.

Information on these excavations is given below and in tables 13.1, 13.2, and 13.3.

### THE RAMON ALLONES HOUSE, LA INSULAR

This house was built c. 1605 and occupied latterly by Ramon Allones, an administrator and, like most of his colleagues, a bachelor. Built of local stone bound with shell mortar and having seven rooms, it can be considered typical of the residences of the Spanish officials. The finds include materials from the midden just outside the back door. The servants' quarters, some distance from the house, have not yet been tested. As in the case of other houses occupied by Europeans, the artifacts have been sorted into groups (following S. South, *Method and Theory in Historical Archaeology* [New York: Academic Press, 1977]) (table 13.1).

The *kitchen* group is self-explanatory; the *architecture* group includes nails, clamps, other construction hardware, and, in this case only, window glass. The *furniture* group contains knobs, hinges, escutcheon plates, and the like; *arms and armor* has guns, in this case matchlock and wheellock parts, gunflints, musket balls, crossbow parts, and bolts, swords, halberds, casques, and so forth. *Clothing* comprises buttons, buckles, thimbles, pins, and the like, while the *personal* group consists of coins, keys, crucifixes, hairbrushes, and other such items. Several Indian personal items were also found in this house; these comprise earspools (fig. 13.4a), beads, pearls, and a silver bracelet that

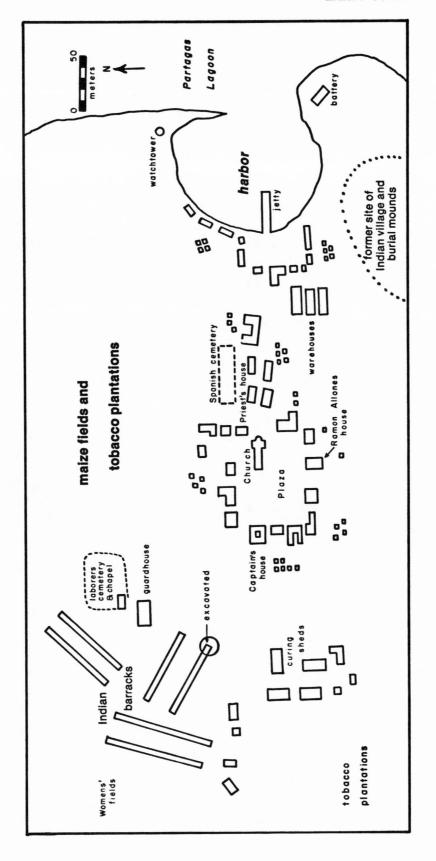

**Figure 13.3. Plan of La Insular**

from its size had probably been worn by a woman. The *tobacco pipes* group includes imported specimens—in Dutch sites these are normally marked "In Gouda," in Spanish sites they are either British or French made—and there are local European-made copies of the imports besides the typical Indian elbow pipes (fig. 13.4b). The *activities* group brings together farm and construction tools and other craft items, harnesses, barrel bands, trade goods, and other miscellaneous hardware.

### THE BARRACKS, LA INSULAR

The barracks housed the Indians working on the tobacco plantations. They were built by their inmates following traditional wattle and daub construction techniques. A two-room section of one of the barracks has been excavated together with its refuse tip, and the finds were studied by a team of specialists in precolonial archaeology. Table 13.2 lists the artifacts from this and other buildings occupied by Indians.

### THE FACTORY, CASTELLA

This trading post, a strong timber construction built in 1627 at the highest point on the Rio Partagas navigable by pinnace, was destroyed by

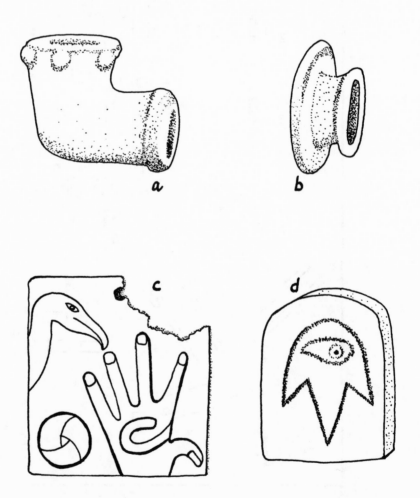

**Figure 13.4.** Artifacts from early colonial sites: a: elbow pipe; b: ear spool; c: engraved copper sheet; d: engraved stone tablet, weeping eye motif

Dutch commandos in 1633. At that time it housed a few Spaniards under the command of a certain Long Pedro. The many flattened musket balls contribute substantially to the high frequency of the arms and armor group. The activities group includes goods for the Indian trade.

### INDIAN HOUSE, CASTELLA

The Macanudo village at Castella consisted of some 20 wattle and daub houses, a small temple mound, and, across the Partagas, a group of burial mounds. The village is believed to have been in existence before the building of the factory. The house was chosen by random sampling.

### FARMHOUSE, DANNEMAN BOERDERIJ

The farmstead appears to have been quite substantial, consisting of a farmhouse, a laborer's cottage, a barn, a byre, a pig pen, and several smaller outhouses. The farmhouse was a four-room brick building. The midden was located 23 meters from the kitchen door. The activities group includes a few toys and a ploughshare.

### LABORER'S COTTAGE, DANNEMAN BOERDERIJ

This was a two-room timber structure occupied by an Indian family in the Danneman's service.

### FORT RITMEESTER

A timber redoubt was enclosed within a ditch and a pentagonal palisade. The fort was occupied only for a short time and was partially disassembled after the defeat of the Spanish.

**TABLE 13.1.** Percentage frequencies of artifacts by groups from European-occupied buildings and associated middens

| ARTIFACTS | LA INSULAR R. ALLONES HOUSE c.1605–33 | CASTELLA FACTORY 1627–33 | DANNEMAN FARM FARMHOUSE c.1591–1610 | FT. RITMEESTER 1630–35 |
|---|---|---|---|---|
| Kitchen group | | | | |
|   Ceramics | | | | |
|     Imported | 40 | 15 | 13 | 4 |
|     Copies of imports | — | — | 25 | 16 |
|     Indian-made | — | 7 | 1 | 2 |
|   Glassware | 14 | 7 | 3 | 8 |
|   Other | 6 | 4 | 8 | 4.5 |
| Architecture group | 17 | 39 | 24 | 43 |
| Furniture group | 2 | 0.5 | 3 | — |
| Arms and Armor | 3 | 8 | 2 | 5 |
| Clothing | 3 | 1 | 3 | 3 |
| Personal items | | | | |
|   European | 1.5 | 1 | 2 | 0.5 |
|   Indian | 2.5 | 0.5 | — | — |
| Tobacco pipes | | | | |
|   Imports | 7 | 8 | — | 5 |
|   Copies of imports | — | — | — | 6 |
|   Elbow pipes | 1 | 4 | 7 | 1 |
| Activities group | 3 | 5 | 9 | 2 |
| Total artifacts | 2137 | 643 | 1918 | 484 |

**TABLE 13.2.  Percentage frequencies of artifacts from buildings occupied by Indians and their associated middens**

| ARTIFACTS | LA INSULAR BARRACKS | CASTELLA INDIAN HOUSE | DANNEMAN FARM LABORER'S COTTAGE |
|---|---|---|---|
| Pottery | | | |
|   Imported | — | 1 | 2 |
|   Copies of imported | — | — | 13 |
|   Indian-made | 46.8 | 32.5 | 19 |
| Stone | | | |
|   Flaked projectile points | 0.5 | 5 | 5 |
|   Scrapers | 6 | 4 | 3 |
|   Plummets, netweights | 1 | 3 | 1.5 |
|   Engraved tablets | — | 1 (fig. 13.4d) | — |
|   Mica sheet frags | — | 1 | 0.2 |
|   Milling stones | 1.2 | 2 | — |
| Bone, Antler, Teeth | | | |
|   Projectile points | — | 3 | 3 |
|   Awls, needles | 4 | 2 | 1.5 |
|   Shoulder-blade hoes | 3 | 2 | — |
|   Shark's tooth chisels | — | 0.5 | — |
|   Buttons | 1 | — | 1 |
|   Flute | — | 0.2 | — |
|   Tortoiseshell rattle | — | 0.1 | — |
| Shell, Pearl | | | |
|   Axes, adzes, chisels | — | 2 | 0.2 |
|   Dippers | 2 | 0.9 | 0.5 |
|   Breast ornaments | — | 1 (fig. 13.4c) | 0.3 |
|   Ear spools | 3 (fig. 13.4b) | 2 | — |
|   Beads | 9.5 | 9 | 2 |
|   Pearls | 0.5 | 4 | 0.5 |
| Metal | | | |
|   Knives, hatchets, axes | 4 | 2.5 | 3 |
|   Agricultural tools | 6 | — | 4 |
|   Other craft eqpt. | 0.5 | 0.5 | 4 |
|   Fish hooks | 0.5 | 3 | 1 |
|   Metal kitchenware | — | 0.2 | 0.3 |
|   Nails, spikes, clamps | 1 | 2 | 29 |
|   Musket balls | — | 5.6 | — |
|   Silver beads | 0.1 | — | — |
|   Engraved copper sheet | — | 1 | — |
| Glass | | | |
|   Beads | 4.4 | 5 | 2 |
|   Bottles, wine or gin | 1 | 3 | 1 |
| Tobacco pipes | | | |
|   Elbow pipes | 5 (fig. 13.4a) | 2 | 3 |
|   Stone effigy pipes | — | 1 | — |
| Total artifacts | 679 | 582 | 484 |

**FAUNA:**    The macrofaunal remains from the excavated buildings and their associated middens have been studied, with the results set out in table 13.3.

TABLE 13.3. Macrofaunal bones from New Frisian early colonial sites: percentage frequencies by species or group. Fish bones and shell present at the riverine sites await analysis.

| FAUNA | LA INSULAR | | CASTELLA | | DANNEMAN BOERDERIJ | | FT. RITMEESTER |
|---|---|---|---|---|---|---|---|
| | ALLONES HOUSE | INDIAN BARRACKS | FACTORY | INDIAN HOUSE | FARMHOUSE | LABORER'S COTTAGE | |
| Domestic | | | | | | | |
| Horse | 6 | 8 | 12 | — | — | — | 1 |
| Cattle | — | — | — | — | 20 | 14 | 56 |
| Sheep | 5 | 8 | — | — | 8 | 9 | — |
| Goat | 5 | 9 | 10 | — | — | — | — |
| Pig | 6 | 8 | 15 | 4 | 22 | 15 | 23 |
| Dog | 5 | 18 | 2 | 12 | 2 | 4 | — |
| Cat | — | — | — | — | 3 | — | — |
| Turkey | 6 | 12 | 6 | 13 | 6 | 7 | — |
| Chicken | 11 | 7 | 3 | — | 12 | 4 | 1 |
| Duck, goose | — | — | — | — | 7 | 1 | — |
| Wild | | | | | | | |
| Deer | 19 | 4 | 8 | 21 | 1 | 9 | 4 |
| Rabbit | 9 | 8 | 5 | 9 | 2 | 9 | 6 |
| Raccoon | 3 | 2 | 6 | 3 | 1 | 6 | 2 |
| Opossum | 2 | 3 | 5 | 4 | 2 | 5 | 1 |
| Alligator | 2 | 3 | 7 | 6 | — | 1 | — |
| Armadillo | — | 4 | — | 5 | — | 1 | — |
| Carnivores | 6 | 1 | 11 | 18 | 3 | 6 | — |
| Wildfowl | 15 | 5 | 10 | 5 | 11 | 9 | 6 |
| Total bones | 592 | 247 | 178 | 473 | 329 | 151 | 164 |

Can you now, on the basis of the archaeological, palaeontological, and historical evidence, suggest answers to the questions raised by Helena Larga? How did the Spanish and Dutch approaches to colonization differ? Did they face different constraints and problems? To what extent is there comparable intersite variation within each immigrant community? How did Spanish-Indian and Dutch-Indian relations differ, and was the colonial impact felt equally by all sections of Indian society?

Steve Daniels was trained at the University of Cambridge. After serving as the Inspector of Monuments in Zambia, he moved to Nigeria where he taught and carried out research for ten years at the Institute of African Studies of the University of Ibadan, and subsequently at its newly founded Department of Archaeology. Ahmadu Bello University in northern Nigeria appointed him to head the Archaeological Statistical Unit, and he developed the AQUA computer program package serving archaeologists throughout the country. He has run his own archaeological computing consultancy in Britain and now works in the Academic Computing Service of the Open University. He is coauthor with Brian Fagan and David Phillipson of a volume on *Iron Age Cultures in Zambia* and has written numerous papers on research design and quantitative methods.

Nicholas David obtained his B.A. at Cambridge and his Ph.D. from Harvard. He has taught at the University of Pennsylvania and University College, London, and was Professor of Archaeology at the University of Ibadan from 1974 to 1978. Following several years' work in Europe on Upper Palaeolithic problems, he directed programs of archaeological and ethnographic research in Cameroon, Nigeria, the Central African Republic, and the Southern Sudan. Besides excavation reports, he has written on a wide variety of topics, including typology, cultural dynamics, ethnoarchaeology and the culture history of West and Central Africa. He is now an Associate Professor of Archaeology at the University of Calgary.